GREAT LIVES OBSERVED

Maria Theresa

Edited by KARL A. ROIDER, JR.

I am only a woman, but I have the heart of a king.

—MARIA THERESA

A SPECTRUM BOOK

PRENTICE-HALL, INC., ENGLEWOOD CLIFFS, N.J.

Library of Congress Cataloging in Publication Data

ROIDER, KARL A   comp.
    Maria Theresa.

    (Great lives observed) (A Spectrum Book)
    CONTENTS: Maria Theresa looks at the world: Conflict with Prussia.
Reforms. Foreign affairs. Family.—Maria Theresa viewed by her contempo-
raries: Voltaire: The brave young queen. [etc.]
    1. Maria Theresia, Empress of Austria, 1717-1780. 2. Austria—History—
Maria Theresa, 1740-1780.
DB71.R6   943′.053′0924 [B]   72-10940
ISBN 0-13-556191-4
ISBN 0-13-556183-3 (pbk)

© 1973 by PRENTICE-HALL, INC.
Englewood Cliffs, New Jersey

A SPECTRUM BOOK

10 9 8 7 6 5 4 3 2 1

Printed in the United States of America

PRENTICE-HALL INTERNATIONAL, INC. (*London*)
PRENTICE-HALL OF AUSTRALIA, PTY. LTD. (*Sydney*)
PRENTICE-HALL OF CANADA, LTD. (*Toronto*)
PRENTICE-HALL OF INDIA PRIVATE LIMITED (*New Delhi*)
PRENTICE-HALL OF JAPAN, INC. (*Tokyo*)

Contents

PART ONE
MARIA THERESA LOOKS AT THE WORLD

1

2

3

4

PART TWO
MARIA THERESA VIEWED BY HER CONTEMPORARIES

22

23

Introduction

In 1740 Maria Theresa, eldest daughter of Holy Roman Emperor Charles VI, became sovereign of the crownlands of the House of Habsburg, the only woman to rule in the 650-year history of that dynasty. Upon ascending to this position, she found the very existence of her heritage threatened by many aggressive neighbors. Her response to these threats laid the foundation for the programs by which her successors transformed their inheritance into a modern state. This achievement guaranteed Maria Theresa a place in the front rank of the dynastic rulers of her era, the age of monarchy when hereditary sovereigns won regard as the most progressive forces in Western civilization.

On approaching the study of Maria Theresa, the modern reader is inevitably impressed and, too often, discouraged by the plethora of strange-sounding places over which she held sway. Maria Theresa's titles in 1774 illustrate the number of lands her house controlled:

By God's Grace, Roman Empress, Widow; queen of Hungary, Bohemia, Dalmatia, Croatia, Slavonia, Galicia, Lodomeria, etc.; archduchess of Austria; duchess of Burgundy, Styria, Carinthia, and Carniola; grand duchess of Transylvania; margravine of Moravia; duchess of Brabant, Limburg, Geldern, Württemberg, Upper and Lower Silesia, Milan, Mantua, Parma, Piacenza, Guastalla, Auschwitz, and Zator; princess of Swabia; princely countess of Habsburg, Flanders, Tyrol, Hennegau, Kyburg, Gorizia, and Gradisza; margravine of the Holy Roman Empire, Burgau, Upper and Lower Lausitz; countess of Namur; mistress of the Windish Mark and Mecheln, etc.; widowed duchess of Lorraine and Bar; grand duchess of Tuscany, etc.

Despite this lengthy list (indeed, the empress only claimed to rule some of these territories), her empire can be divided into five basic sections: the Austrian lands including Upper Austria, Lower Austria, the Tyrol, and Inner Austria, most of which form part of present-day Austria; the Bohemian lands, including Bohemia and Moravia in modern Czechoslovakia and the duchy of Silesia, most of which Prussia wrested from Austria in 1740; the Italian possessions,

1

including Milan and Tuscany; Hungary, including Transylvania, Croatia, and the military frontier; and the western provinces, including modern Belgium and a variety of German possessions known as the Vorlände.

To understand the reign of Maria Theresa, one must be aware of the disparities among these lands, for she devoted most of her life to the tasks of retaining them and reforming the government that ruled them. The modern reader must not imagine these territories as one state united by a common constitution, language, or legal tradition because virtually no bond existed among them aside from the person of the ruler. Each land possessed its own laws, customs, and history and negotiated individually with the Habsburg monarch to determine its financial and military obligations. It fell to the sovereign alone to direct them toward a unified policy for their joint defense and preservation. And no Habsburg achieved so much success in this work as did Maria Theresa, but even she encountered obstacles that could not be overcome. Her famous reforms, for example, were implemented for the most part only in the Austrian and Bohemian lands; Hungary was infrequently included and the Italian and western lands not at all.

These reforms became necessary because of the succession crisis that confronted Maria Theresa when she ascended the throne. Prior to her rule, only males were recognized as legal heirs in the Habsburg dynasty, and after 1711 her father was the last male Habsburg. Fearing that he might not father a son, Charles, in 1713, made public a document known as the Pragmatic Sanction, which guaranteed the right of succession to his daughters. It was a wise precaution, for after producing a son who lived only a few months, Charles and his wife had only daughters. When his fears had been realized, Charles worked from 1720 to 1725 at persuading his crownlands to accept formally the Pragmatic Sanction, and then for the next ten years he sought similar recognition from the major states of Europe. But certain powers refused his request: the ruler of Bavaria, who coveted Habsburg territory, never submitted his guarantee of female succession, and France offered its approval only under conditions which, if broadly interpreted, meant no recognition at all. Consequently, when Charles died in October, 1740, there remained the danger that some power might challenge the right of his heirs to the Habsburg throne.

To the surprise of the Austrians, the challenge came first not from Bavaria or France, but from Prussia. Although his father had recognized the Pragmatic Sanction, the new king of that country, Frederick II, later called the Great, used the occasion of Charles's death to occupy Silesia, the province closest to the Prussian border and the wealthiest of the Habsburg lands. After Frederick had defeated the meager Austrian army sent to protect Silesia, Bavaria and France joined him by invading Maria Theresa's lands from the west and by installing the elector of Bavaria, Charles Albert, as king of Bohemia (1741) and Holy Roman emperor (1742).

These developments had a profound—indeed lifelong—impact upon Maria Theresa. To save her heritage, she discovered that she could rely upon little except her own endurance, judgment, and strength of character. During the last seven years of her father's reign, the monarchy had been involved in two unfortunate wars which had left the treasury depleted and the army severely weakened. Furthermore, Charles had mistakenly believed that as empress, his daughter would surrender true power to her husband, Francis Stephen of Lorraine; therefore, he took no pains to instruct her in the workings of government. Compounding her lack of knowledge of affairs of state, Maria Theresa inherited from her father a set of advisers who were overaged, unenterprising, jealous of each other, and incapable of offering her the encouragement and counsel she needed. Summing up these liabilities, she wrote in her later years that, upon ascending the throne, she found herself "without money, without credit, without an army, without experience, and finally without advice."

Notwithstanding the discouraging prospects, Maria Theresa resolved at the very beginning not to surrender to her enemies, but to reconquer her lost lands and forge a government capable of resisting all future aggressors. In 1742 she directed her forces into Bavaria, where they captured Munich, the capital, and for the next three years, kept Charles Albert and his French allies on the defensive. Although the Bavarians abandoned the struggle in 1745, the Austrians, having by this time secured allies in Britain, Sardinia, and various German states, fought the French until 1748, when all parties involved agreed to end the struggle by the Treaty of Aix-la-Chapelle.

From the beginning, however, Maria Theresa viewed Prussia rather than Bavaria or France as her foremost enemy; after all, the Prussian king had precipitated the despoilation of the Habsburg lands and had most damaged the prestige of Austrian arms. From 1741 to 1745 he had inflicted frequent defeats upon the Austrians and had twice compelled Maria Theresa to sign treaties ceding Silesia to him. To someone of Maria Theresa's determination, propriety, and sense of duty to her family, Frederick's "rape" of Silesia could not go unpunished, and after 1745 she set out to uproot the weaknesses in her state and prepare it for the next conflict with this "monster" of the north.

Since the most important task involved strengthening the army, Maria Theresa first inquired of her military advisers how many men would be considered adequate to defend her realm. Accepting their estimate of 110,000—50,000 more than in Charles's day—she then asked her ministers to submit proposals for financing such a force. She accepted the plan put forth by Frederick William Haugwitz, an official in the Silesian administration, who in 1741 had arrived in Vienna a practically destitute refugee. Haugwitz's plan provided not only for revenues sufficient to support the new army but also called for a complete reordering of the time-honored system by which the Habsburg monarchs secured money from their crownlands.

Before Maria Theresa's reforms, each province was ruled by an Estate, a parliament in which sat representatives of the local nobility, clergy, and the important towns. These Estates enjoyed many privileges, the most important being the right to negotiate annually with the monarch's representatives to determine the taxes, army recruits, and military supplies their province would owe for the coming year. This system was full of difficulties for the sovereign because, not only did the Estates do their best to keep their dues low, but, since they also collected the taxes, they frequently defaulted on payments, contracted enormous debts of their own, and engaged in all sorts of corrupt practices. To abolish this system and insure the crown a predictable annual income, Haugwitz proposed to secure the Estates' approval of taxes only every ten years, to levy dues on the previously nontaxable noble land, and to organize a centralized office to assist in tax collection.

Despite tremendous opposition to Haugwitz's plan, Maria Theresa endorsed it and in January, 1748, signed it into law. This reform much improved the Habsburg financial structure and did provide the funds needed to establish the standing army at its recommended strength. After implementation of the new system the Estates themselves, although never formally abolished, lost virtually all of their influence and from then on led only a shadow existence.

This first major reform proved to be only the beginning of sweeping changes that affected virtually every aspect of administration, from the local counties to the highest central organs of the state. By the time of Maria Theresa's death, the government was far more centralized, efficient, and effective than it had been under her predecessors, and it gave the monarchy a measure of unity more meaningful and reliable than such documents as the Pragmatic Sanction. Admittedly, Haugwitz's innovations did not remain untouched during Maria Theresa's reign; many offices were created, abolished, manipulated, and renamed. Nonetheless, despite such frequent changes, the goal of the empress and her ministers was always the extension of the authority of the central government.

By 1756 Maria Theresa judged her state sufficiently strong to renew her struggle with Frederick II for possession of Silesia. First, however, she had to create a general European diplomatic situation that would favor Austria during the hostilities. To perform this task, the empress possessed a valuable assistant in Wenzel Anthony Kaunitz, a remarkably astute individual who had served as ambassador to France from 1751 to 1753 and then as Maria Theresa's chief adviser in foreign affairs. Kaunitz first came to the empress's attention in 1749 when, in response to a general query about future Austrian foreign policy, he suggested that the state abandon its traditional alliance with Britain and try to secure an accord with its long-time enemy France. Although recent scholarship has shown that this idea was by no means new in Habsburg policy-making, Kaunitz and Maria Theresa made it a reality. The right conditions for this reversal of alliances developed in 1756, when Britain and Prussia reached a joint agreement (the Convention of Westminster) and thereby inspired Austria and France to do the same. Shortly thereafter Russia joined the Austro-French coalition, effectively preventing Prussia's having any powerful friends on the Continent.

Aware of the dangers posed by the alliance of Austria, Russia, and France, in August, 1756, Frederick invaded Saxony, one of Austria's allies, in the hope that his surprise action would undermine the newly created coalition. Frederick's attack did disconcert his enemies at first, but by 1757, recovered from their initial perplexity, they promised not to abandon each other and engaged the Prussians in earnest.

This conflict, known as the Seven Years' War, represents Maria Theresa's supreme effort to defeat her archenemy and to recover Silesia. Indeed, on numerous occasions it appeared that she would: in June, 1757, for example, the Habsburg armies achieved their first major victory over Frederick at Kolin and shortly thereafter occu-

pied coveted Silesia; in October, 1758, they won again at Hochkirch
and in August, 1759, inflicted such a crushing defeat on Frederick
at Kunersdorf that Berlin, the Prussian capital, was exposed to raids
by the Russians. None of these successes proved decisive, however,
for the Austrians persistently failed to take full advantage of them
and Frederick repeatedly regrouped his forces and struck back, sometimes scoring remarkable victories of his own. By 1761 neither side
had brought the other to its knees, and in January, 1762, the death
of the empress of Russia and succession of her pro-Prussian nephew
marked the end of Russian participation in the war. Thereafter,
Maria Theresa engaged in one last summer of fighting before admit-
ting that continuing the war would prove fruitless. Finally in 1763
she signed the Treaty of Hubertusberg, ending hostilities and recog-
nizing Prussian possession of Silesia as permanent.

Much speculation has surrounded the effects of Austria's loss of
Silesia. Many historians argue that the wealth and predominantly
German population of this province gave Prussia the resources it
needed to unify Germany under its hegemony in the nineteenth century. Had Silesia remained Austrian, the Habsburgs might have
unified Germany under their own sceptre or at least prevented it
from falling to the Prussians. Even had Austria not united Germany,
some scholars maintain that the presence of the Silesian Germans
in the western portion of the monarchy would have assured German
dominance in that area and would have done much to minimize the
nationalities' strife that infected Austria in the late nineteenth and
early twentieth centuries.

Our purpose here is not to resolve these issues, but to emphasize
that Maria Theresa considered them unimportant. She wished to
reconquer Silesia not because of its Germanness, but because it was
a hereditary province of economic importance. She did not regard
her struggle with Frederick as the first Austro-Prussian war for control of the Germanies, but as a dynastic effort to right the wrong that
he had inflicted upon her house.

Although she frequently spoke of her fondness for the Germans,
Maria Theresa by no means considered herself a German national-
ist, and the life of her court did not reflect a German bias. When
writing to her friends and family, she preferred French; however,
she used a distinctly German style of sentence structure that makes
her letters somewhat difficult for French students to read. In speaking she usually employed German—except when talking with her
husband, who knew little German—but with a broad Viennese ac-

cent that became the butt of many humorous anecdotes. Her court was international and therefore multilingual; an early nineteenth-century author Caroline Pichler reported that her mother, one of Maria Theresa's ladies-in-waiting, had to know four languages— French, Italian, German, and Latin—simply to be able to read to the empress. This same author wrote that, among the courtiers and ministers, other languages were preferred to German because they were regarded as more elegant. To illustrate her point, she cited an eighteenth-century Viennese ditty that ran:

> I speak Italian like Dante,
> Latin like Cicero,
> English like Pope and Thompson,
> Greek like Demosthenes,
> French like Diderot,
> and German like my wet nurse.

Maria Theresa was first and foremost a Habsburg, and no loyalty superseded her devotion to her line.

In 1765, just two years after the conclusion of the Seven Years' War, Maria Theresa suffered a much more crushing disappointment than the loss of Silesia—the unexpected death of her husband, Francis Stephen of Lorraine. All her adult life, she had been deeply in love with him, and his passing affected her noticeably. From 1765 until her own death in 1780, she dressed in mourning, spent hours each week in prayer, and spoke frequently of her grief at his absence.

Indeed, except for her duty to the state, throughout her lifetime she regarded nothing as more important than devotion to her family. Aware of the misfortune heaped on her house because of its scarcity of heirs, she made certain, by giving birth to five boys and eleven girls, that it would never again suffer a lack of offspring. As she wrote to one of her daughters, "I can never have enough children; in this I am insatiable." After the death of her husband one of her gladdest moments came in 1768 when she received word of the birth of her first grandson, thus assuring the succession in the male line for another generation. The eldest son Joseph II had married, but his first and dearly beloved wife had died three years after the wedding and he refused to love again, thus leaving the burden of providing heirs to his younger brother Leopold. Leopold and his wife complied in grand fashion, however, producing twelve children —eight of them boys.

In her attitude toward her husband and her family, Maria Theresa was solicitous, in fact, downright bossy. She was extremely jealous of her husband and resented any pleasantries he showed to other women at court. Despite her love for Francis Stephen, she never allowed him a decisive voice in affairs of state and occasionally dismissed him from council meetings if he expressed a point-of-view contrary to her own.

Regarding her children, throughout her life she remained a concerned mother, offering recommendations and giving advice to each even after they had reached adulthood. In the best tradition of ruling houses, the spouses of her children, especially the daughters, were selected to cement alliances or to assure the friendship of foreign states. Some of the marriages were happy, others were not; but regardless of her childrens' contentment or lack thereof, Maria Theresa advised all of them to love their husbands and wives and to do nothing to lose their affection. Throughout her later years, she avoided as much as possible using her childrens' positions to influence the policies of foreign courts, and she warned her sons and daughters against telling her any secrets they kept from their spouses.

Of her offspring, her favorite was Joseph II, the eldest son who became emperor and coregent upon the death of his father and who succeeded to full sovereignty after Maria Theresa's passing in 1780. A strong-willed, arrogant, but able man, Joseph chafed under the restrictions his mother placed on his authority during their coregency, and their frequent quarrels became famous.

In her voluminous letters to Joseph and the rest of her children, Maria Theresa revealed her beliefs and feelings concerning the major trends of thought in the eighteenth century. Although deeply religious and totally committed to Roman Catholicism, she had no misconceptions about the abuses in the church of her day. She severely restricted her own gifts to the church, commenting that the clergy misused the property they already possessed, and she advised her children against being overly generous to priests and monastic orders. Furthermore, she had no qualms about removing church influence from education, remarking that the state could better train citizens for their proper roles in society. Nonetheless, she could not bear the thought of tolerating Protestantism and complained bitterly when the pope abolished the Jesuit order in 1773.

Unlike her archrival Frederick, she had no use whatsoever for the prevailing ideas of the Enlightenment and complained that its emphasis on liberty and freedom constituted nothing but a camouflage for license and disorder. She disliked reading and supposedly never read a secular work for enjoyment. The lack of an authoritative religion and morality, she cautioned her children, would lead only to depravity, doubt, and in her eyes worst of all—the damnation of the soul.

After Francis Stephen's death, Maria Theresa became increasingly withdrawn, but she by no means lost her vigor. Reforms continued at a slower but more systematic pace, and her foreign policy aimed not to recover Silesia but to maintain peace and preserve the status quo. The empress had not lost her will to fight, but having experienced the enormous frustrations and sacrifices of fifteen years of war, she was considerably more reluctant to embark on adventures that might prove unsuccessful.

Like her foreign policy, Maria Theresa's reforms in this later period also took on a different character. Although still instituted primarily to strengthen the state, they focused less on strictly financial and administrative improvements and more on human concerns, like education, civil and criminal law, and most important, the alleviation of the depressed condition of the peasants. As in most eastern European states in the eighteenth century, the peasants were largely unfree serfs, owing their lords a wide variety of work and money dues. In addition, they had to pay most of the direct taxes to the state, give a tenth of their income to the church, and provide soldiers for the army. Although some of the peasants in the western portion of the monarchy were relatively well off, those in the east, particularly in Hungary and Bohemia, suffered severely from the excessive demands of their lords. Maria Theresa first became aware of the peasants' plight in 1764, when, angered by the Hungarian Estates' refusal to reduce the peasants' dues so that they might pay higher taxes to the state, she began to investigate the condition of serfs in Hungary. Similar investigations in other provinces plus occasional outbursts of peasant violence inspired the empress to issue reforms in virtually every crownland that limited the work dues the peasants owed their lords. Furthermore, she experimented with changes on her own properties, including the implementation of a plan to give the peasants title to the land they plowed in exchange for lifelong cash rents, thus abolishing work dues altogether. Undoubtedly the practical motives of improving the peasants' ability to pay taxes and preventing peasant revolution prompted Maria Theresa to implement these innovations, but a fundamental humanitarianism and sense of justice certainly played a role in convincing her of the need to alleviate her subjects' oppression.

Despite these reforms, Maria Theresa never considered altering the essential fabric of society. She believed in the hierarchical social structure of eighteenth-century Europe and was quite convinced that a nobleman was truly a better man than a commoner. But, as in most matters, she did not allow this attitude to interfere with her fundamentally pragmatic approach to reforms, and she did not mind authorizing changes that curtailed the influence of the great landed aristocracy.

From 1765 to 1780 family problems and reform occupied most of Maria Theresa's time. Of course, foreign policy concerns persisted, but aside from the Polish partition in 1772 and the War of the Bavarian Succession in 1778, they assumed much less significance than in the first years of her reign. By her death in 1780 Maria Theresa's tasks were essentially complete: the government was stable, Austrian power was respected in Europe, the condition of her subjects was improved, and the House of Habsburg (now officially Habsburg-Lorraine) was revitalized by an abundance of offspring. During her life and after her death a number of sobriquets were suggested to honor her, but she remained simply Maria Theresa, one of the greatest monarchs of the eighteenth century.

In the following pages, Maria Theresa presents her own views on the issues of government and family life, and some of her contemporaries offer their opinions about her at different times during her reign. In the last part, historians have their say, and in doing so, express a variety of opinions that add to the complexity and fascination of this remarkable woman.

Chronology of the Life of Maria Theresa

1713	Publication of Pragmatic Sanction by Charles VI.
1717	(May 13) Birth of Maria Theresa.
1720–25	Crownlands of the House of Habsburg guarantee the Pragmatic Sanction.
1732	Diet of the Holy Roman Empire, at the inisistence of Frederick William I, King of Prussia, recognizes the Pragmatic Sanction as imperial law, binding on all the Germanies. Bavaria refuses to comply.
1733–35	War of the Polish Succession.
1736	(February 12) Marriage of Maria Theresa to Francis Stephen of Lorraine.
1737–39	War with the Turks.
1737	(February 5) Birth of first daughter, Elizabeth (died 1740).
1738	(October 6) Birth of second daughter, Maria Anna.
1739	(September 18) Treaty of Belgrade ends Turkish War.
1740	(January 1) Birth of third daughter, Caroline (died 1741). (October 20) Death of Charles VI, succession of Maria Theresa. (December 16) Prussian invasion of Silesia results in first Silesian War
1741	(March 13) Birth of first son, Joseph. (April 10) Prussian victory over Austria at Battle of Mollwitz. (June 25) Coronation as queen of Hungary. (September 11) Appearance before Hungarian Diet. (November 26) Franco-Bavarian conquest of Prague.
1742	(January 23) Election of Charles Albert of Bavaria as Holy Roman emperor. (February 14) Austrian occupation of Munich. Alliance with Britain. (May 13) Birth of fourth daughter, Maria Christine. (June 11) Preliminary Peace of Breslau cedes Silesia to Prussia. (July 28) Definitive Peace of Berlin cedes Silesia to Prussia.
1743	(June 27) British victory over French at Battle of Dettingen. (August 13) Birth of fifth daughter, Elizabeth. Coronation as queen of Bohemia.
1744	Second Silesian War—Frederick reopens hostilities and occupies Prague.
1745	(January 20) Death of Charles Albert, Holy Roman emperor. (February 1) Birth of second son, Charles Joseph (died 1761).

	(October 4) Coronation of Francis Stephen of Lorraine as Holy Roman emperor. (December 25) Peace of Dresden with Prussia ends second Silesian War.
1746	(February 26) Birth of sixth daughter, Maria Amalia.
1746–56	First reform period.
1747	(May 5) Birth of third son, Leopold.
1748	(January 29) Adoption of Haugwitz's plan for ten years' recess of the Estates. (September 17) Birth of seventh daughter, Caroline (died 1748). (October 23) Treaty of Aix-la-Chapelle ends war with France.
1749	(May 2) Abolition of Austrian and Bohemian chancellories and creation of General Directory.
1750	(February 4) Birth of eighth daughter, Joanna.
1751	(March 19) Birth of ninth daughter, Josepha.
1752–53	Reform and secularization of University of Vienna.
1752	(August 13) Birth of tenth daughter, Maria Caroline.
1753	Establishment of state censorship over all religious and political publications.
1754	(June 1) Birth of fourth son, Ferdinand.
1755	(November 2) Birth of eleventh daughter, Marie Antoinette.
1756	(January 16) Convention of Westminster establishes Prusso-British accord. (May 1) First Treaty of Versailles creates Austro-French alliance. (August 29) Seven Years' War begins with Prussian invasion of Saxony. (December 18) Birth of fifth son, Maximilian.
1757	(May) Offensive alliances signed with France and Russia. (June 18) Austrian victory over Frederick at Kolin. (November 5) Victory of Frederick over a combined Austro-French army at Rossbach. (December 5) Victory of Frederick over Austrians at Leuthen.
1758	(October 14) Austrian victory at Hochkirch.
1759	(August 12) Austro-Russian victory over Frederick at Kunersdorf.
1761	(January 26) Creation of state council.
1761–78	Second reform period.
1762	(January 5) Death of Empress Elizabeth of Russia and subsequent withdrawal of Russia from war.
1763	(February 8) Treaty of Hubertusberg ends Seven Years' War on basis of *status quo ante bellum*.
1765	(August 8) Death of Francis Stephen of Lorraine. (September) Joseph crowned Holy Roman emperor and appointed coregent.
1767	Maria Theresa suffers from smallpox. (January 26) Serf reform issued for Hungary.

1769–72	Crisis over Poland.
1771	Model serf reform (*Robot Patent*) issued for Austrian Silesia.
1772	(August 5) First partition of Poland.
1774	School reform introduced in Austria and Bohemia.
1775	Serf reform (*Robot Patent*) issued for Bohemia.
1778–79	War of the Bavarian Succession (the Potato War).
1779	(May 13) Treaty of Teschen ends War of the Bavarian Succession.
1780	(November 29) Death of Maria Theresa.

MARIA THERESA LOOKS AT THE WORLD

During her life Maria Theresa wrote much, not in the form of well-conceived and closely argued justifications of her policies, but in bustling letters and memoranda to her ministers, friends, and family. The only comprehensive political tract of the empress's own creation was her Political Testament, a document apparently dictated to her secretaries during the winter of 1749–50 and addressed "for the special use of my posterity." Despite its confusing style and erratic shifts of subject matter, the Testament provides the most valuable insight into Maria Theresa's own judgment of those difficult early years of conflict and change. In all her writing, whether discussing affairs of state or personal matters, she reveals a fascinating mixture of common sense and heartfelt emotion, traits that made her one of the most successful and, at the same time, best-loved monarchs of her age.

1

Conflict with Prussia

Undoubtedly the dominating element of Maria Theresa's long reign was the challenge posed by Frederick the Great. From Frederick's conquest of Silesia in 1740–41 to the end of the Seven Years' War in 1763, the empress's internal and external policies focused upon strengthening her state and creating a favorable diplomatic situation for the defeat of the Prussian monarch and recovery of the lost province. After 1763, although her enthusiasm for war had declined noticeably, most of her attention in foreign affairs continued to reflect her bitter rivalry with the king of Prussia.

WEAKNESS OF HER REALM

In this selection from the first several pages of her Political Testament, *Maria Theresa discusses the problems she faced on ascending the throne and suffering the invasion of Silesia. Her recollections of those days indicate that her most pressing problems lay in securing the necessary advice from her counselors and the means from her crownlands to resist. Of particular notice are her complaints about the provincial loyalty of some of her chief ministers and the confusion in the Austrian administrative structure.*[1]

The unexpected tragic death of my lord father of holy memory filled me with great grief because not only did I love and honor him as a father, but like the least of his subjects, considered him my sovereign. Furthermore, I felt double the loss and pain because I possessed so little familiarity with affairs of state and so little knowledge necessary to rule such extensive and diverse lands, and my father had never been inclined to instruct me as to the discharge of either foreign or domestic affairs. Consequently, I saw myself stripped all at once of money, soldiers, and advice.

At that time, having had no practice in selecting councilors and being timid and insecure because of it, I had great difficulty assessing the suggestions and instructions offered to me. In the last ten unfortunate years of my father's reign, I had only heard, like any private person, the misfortunes and laments that reached the public, without knowing their origins or why they came. At that time, unlike today, everything was not revealed openly to all the ministers, but kept secret. I resolved, therefore, not to conceal my ignorance but to listen to each official in his own department and thus inform myself correctly. Count [Louis Philip] Sinzendorf, the court chancellor [responsible for foreign affairs], was a great statesman and I realized his loss only later, but at that time I did not fully trust him. Count [Gundaker Thomas] Starhemberg [minister of finance] possessed my complete confidence, and I revered him very much, although he lacked the great political insight of Sinzendorf. From the beginning, the court chancellor prepared me and informed me

[1] Alfred von Arneth, ed., "Zwei Denkschriften der Kaiserin Maria Theresia," *Archiv für österreichische Geschichte*, XLVII (1871), 285–94. Translated by the editor.

of everything, but Starhemberg enjoyed my thorough trust. This situation continued quite smoothly until the arrival of [Philip Joseph] Kinsky [Bohemian court chancellor], who, albeit with the best intentions, caused me such confusion and perplexity that I lost my even temper and became greatly depressed.

At this time I received [John Christopher] Bartenstein, recommended to me by Counts Starhemberg and [Ferdinand Leopold] Herberstein. Although at first strongly prejudiced against him, I soon found him, as everyone acquainted with him will testify, a great statesman and thereafter often used him to settle my quarrels in council and to speak to one minister or another. Nonetheless, all this talk only caused me more disquiet so that, contrary to my character, I frequently became indecisive and distrustful. Had God himself not interfered by causing all these men to die, I would never have been able to remedy the situation because I would rather have injured myself than taken a violent step that would have damaged the honor and reputation of another. This feeling is easy to understand, for my biases toward them were my personal prejudices, and I am sure the ministers all meant well, but they simply did not want to cooperate, mostly out of ambition and a desire to have more influence than others. Certainly these men influenced policy, but in major decisions they never prevented me from contradicting them. In all these affairs Bartenstein supported me completely, using his knowledge of dealing with men, and serving me so well with his counsel and information that he won my confidence, which he never abused; he became my principal adviser as my reign began.

From the beginning I decided that, as my principles, I would depend upon my own forthright intentions and prayers to God; I would remove myself from all minor worries, arrogance, personal ambition, and other emotions—which I have on occasion observed in myself—and I would undertake all the necessary business of government resolutely and without passion. These maxims, with the help of God, have sustained me in my great difficulties and have made me stand firm by my decisions. In all my acts—those done and those left undone—I have chosen as my highest rule a trust in God, who, without regard to my own desires, has chosen me for this position and will make me worthy of it through my deeds, principles, and intentions. Thus I felt able to solicit His help and win His almighty protection for myself and my subjects; I recalled this truth daily and it reminded me that I was responsible not only to myself but to my people.

Having each time tested my ideas by these standards, I undertook everything thereafter with complete confidence, sustained mightily and yet so calmly in my soul even in great emergencies, as if they did not affect me personally. With complete tranquillity and pleasure, I would have even abandoned my whole right to rule and surrendered to my enemies, had Divine Providence so willed and had I believed it my duty or the best policy for my lands. And even though I love my heritage and my children and would spare no diligence, worry, concern, or work for them, still, when convinced in my own mind or by general conditions that it is necessary, I would always put the general welfare of my lands first because I am the foremost and universal mother of all my subjects.

In these circumstances, I found myself without money, without credit, without an army, without experience or knowledge, and finally without advice because every counselor wanted to wait and see what would happen. Such were the conditions when my lands were attacked by the king of Prussia. This monarch's sweet words and vigorous promises convinced each of my ministers that he would avoid opening hostilities. This belief—cherished by my ministers, especially Sinzendorf—plus my own inexperience and good faith were the main reasons why defensive preparations in Silesia were neglected, even to the point of failing to muster nearby regiments, and the king of Prussia was given a free hand to conquer the duchy within six weeks.

While the king of Prussia stood before Glogau and would shortly become master of Breslau, he sent [Gustav Adolph] Gotter to me to propose that I give him Silesia in exchange for his assistance in resisting all claims against my succession and especially in securing support for the election of my husband to the imperial crown. A few of my ministers—notably Sinzendorf, [Frederick Augustus] Harrach, and Kinsky—advised me to negotiate a treaty with the king, but others—Starhemberg and Bartenstein, as I recollect— maintained that the surrender of any piece of land, even a few minor principalities, would put the Pragmatic Sanction in great danger because the signatory powers would be less inclined to honor additional guarantees after we ourselves had broken the agreement by signing a treaty with Prussia. Besides, as soon as the king had formally received part of Silesia, he would undoubtedly demand the rest or a great part of the rest as an indemnity for his aid. The result proved us correct: the king wanted all of Silesia.

The misfortune was that, after my firm resolution to resist Prus-

sia's unjust attack with a righteous counterattack, discord and factionalism immediately struck root among my ministers, a result that
developed only from my own naive resolution to do good to all and
to believe that everyone would do his best for me. I wish to God
that I had remained alone with Sinzendorf, Starhemberg, and
Bartenstein; then so many mistakes might have been avoided. I
must explain myself further in this matter: Sinzendorf was a greater
statesman than Starhemberg, but he was not free from prejudices,
ulterior motives, or passions. Although nothing could be proven
against him while he served me, his conduct regarding Prussia was
somewhat irregular, and the warnings I received concerning him
prompted me to put my complete trust in Starhemberg, who was a
greater man and a true German. To be sure, he had not forgotten
that Sinzendorf had won more influence than he over my father and
therefore sought to win the upper hand over me, but Starhemberg
never did so in a way that was dishonest or smacked of intrigue.
He and Herberstein, at that time my master of the household and
and a thoroughly honorable and capable man, introduced me to
Bartenstein; I disliked him at the beginning of my reign but I must
say that he alone was responsible for maintaining this monarchy.
Without Bartenstein all would have been lost because Starhemberg
was no longer as active as he once had been. I learned long afterward that Bartenstein was the only one who prevented my marriage
with the Spanish royal house (which Sinzendorf supported, by the
way), that he alone worked for and sustained the coregency [of
Maria Theresa and her husband, Francis Stephen of Lorraine], advised the marriage of my sister [Maria Anna to the empress's beloved
brother-in-law Charles of Lorraine], and sought to procure all that
assured the unity and strength of my line, which was, after all, the
foundation of this monarchy. I do not say that he lacked failings,
but these were personal in nature and certainly did not grow out of
ambition or from a lack of loyalty or zeal. Of this I am certain and
have a responsibility to proclaim it for his sake and the sake of his
family and descendants. All this I have had to write for my own
satisfaction, in order to give justice to my three ministers, especially
since all the problems grew only from their disagreements and not
from any individual's malice.

    In the first difficult years of my reign, I could not personally ex-
amine the condition and strength of my lands; therefore I had to
rely on the advice of my ministers, who, pretending that any de-

mands upon the populace would make my regime hateful from the outset, suggested that I should ask for neither soldiers nor money from my provinces. Consequently, no funds were forthcoming which could have mobilized a few regiments to march against Prussia. And when I was obliged to solicit private individuals for a few hundred thousand [gulden] as state loans or subsidies, I must note that the most powerful men—even some ministers themselves—tried openly to exempt their own resources.

Especially responsible, although unwittingly, for the indifferent and half-hearted defensive preparations was the Bohemian Chancellor Kinsky, who appealed to my good nature and convinced me (and this is a fact) that the Bohemians were always subordinated to the Austrians. He then overwhelmed me with such arguments and presented so many old figures and documents that I admitted him, against all good counsel, into my close circle of advisers in order to appear the true mother of all my peoples.

Scarcely had I done this, when the vehemence of Kinsky's temperament fully revealed itself. At the beginning I thought that I could contain him, but, despite my hopes, it became evident that he was openly prejudiced for Bohemia, which he strove to favor exclusively. He spoke out for those lands in his trust and attacked all the others, and under the guise of favoring an ideal balance between the Bohemian and Austrian crownlands, arranged that the latter would pay more and the former less.

Here began the real divisions among ministers, bureaucrats, and peoples, which I did not recognize soon enough and which, after it had gone too far, I did not crush severely enough. Because of my good nature—and the delicacy of the situation—I employed half-measures that only made things worse. This was indeed the beginning of all the misfortunes, for although I must attest to Kinsky's honor and loyalty, it is certain that his temperament, vehemence, passion, and parochialism were the true spoilers of all our efforts and that they forced Kinsky himself to act contrary to his own best interests. Even when the war spread to the Bohemian lands, he did not want too many troops to enter the country, believing all the time that we could easily defeat the Prussians. Furthermore, the transfer of some weak regiments stationed on the Turkish and Transylvanian borders proceeded very slowly, owing to his inadequate preparations in the Bohemian provinces.

Conditions became increasingly worse, and because of the division

among the crownlands, no minister had any idea how to extract me
and the state from this dreadful situation. Virtually every suggestion
that implied even the slightest sacrifice from a province was immediately opposed by the minister responsible for the province
affected. Each official cared only for his own interests, and I at that
time lacked the understanding necessary to oppose these men.

[Louis Andrew] Khevenhüller and [Reinhard William] Neipperg
were suggested as commanding generals to oppose the Prussians, but
only the former demanded sufficient regiments and the money necessary to pay the troops their due wages. Being in charge of providing
for the army, Kinsky preferred Neipperg and refused to have anything to do with Khevenhüller. Consequently, I sanctioned Neipperg's appointment, especially since no one found fault with his
military experience.

This officer seemed satisfied with a few weak regiments, which,
along with their generals, he personally selected. It happened that
some of these regiments were called from far away while others,
much nearer to the theater of combat, were left in their quarters.

I flattered myself into expecting that the close harmony between
the commander in chief and the chancellor assigned to supply the
army would bring success, but soon my confidence was shattered.

Although Neipperg had only 14,000 troops under his command,
he believed this number would suffice. Besides, to mobilize more
regiments would have required more taxes from the crownlands,
and Kinsky, through some unbelievable misjudgment, insisted that
no additional demands could be made upon the provinces without
ruining them. Another possible source of troops was the army on the
Turkish frontier, but even though Count [Corfiz Anthony] Uhlfeld
assured us from Turkey that we had nothing to fear, the ministers
did not completely trust the newly established peace nor did they
trust the Hungarians, so they opposed withdrawing too many troops
from the Ottoman frontier.

In general, it was assumed that Neipperg's few soldiers could
contain the inexperienced Prussians.

A few ministers never strayed from their primary view that, regardless of the outcome of events in Silesia, we should sit down and
negotiate with Prussia at the first opportunity. Our expectation that
we could defeat Prussia was actually quite justified because we
hoped to acquire aid from Saxony and Hanover and possibly even
from Russia.

Help from Hanover and Saxony might indeed have come, had we undertaken the war in Silesia with more strength and better planning, but such resolution was impossible because of the above-mentioned indifference of the ministers.

I began to appreciate the mistakes committed by the ministers in my father's reign, but although I tried to read the thoughts of each one, my inexperience prevented me from openly opposing them in important affairs. Instead I tried to smooth over factionalism and achieve as much agreement as possible. Although I did not always succeed—in fact, sometimes did just the opposite—I did try to achieve unity in the most important deliberations.

Actually these aggravating inconveniences were unavoidable because, according to the constitution, every minister served essentially as the lord and master of his department. Consequently, each man possessed so much power that he followed only those policies he thought proper or that agreed with his preconceived notions.

This abuse, which had grown such strong roots for so long a time, was immediately recognizable in all departments, but no matter how hard I fought against it, all was in vain, and the situation at that time prevented me from thoroughly uprooting it.

During my father's reign these ministers were for the most part held in great respect both at home and abroad; their long service had given them much experience and had won for them the admiration and trust of the people. I needed their experience, and they were, by and large, venerable ministers and meritorious and honorable men. At that time I could not dispense with them without making things still worse, so I did not try immediately to limit their excessive authority. The situation made it necessary to postpone my changes until a more opportune time.

DETERMINATION TO PERSEVERE

As implied in the last selection, Austria's initial effort in the first year of the War of the Austrian Succession ended in misfortune. Not only did Neipperg suffer defeat at the hands of the Prussians at the battle of Mollwitz in April, 1741, but in November of that year a combined force of French, Bavarian, and Saxon troops occupied portions of Austria and Bohemia and captured the important city of Prague. At this bleak moment in Habsburg history, Maria Theresa wrote to her Bo-

hemian chancellor, Count Kinsky, emphasizing her resolution
not to give in to the enemies about her.[2]

So Prague is lost, and the consequences will be even worse if
we do not try to provision the troops for another three months. It
is unthinkable to extract any more sacrifices from the Austrian
lands, and nothing can be procured from Hungary for at least three
months, and even then that is uncertain. Finally, Kinsky, the moment has come for everyone to show his courage in order to protect
his land and his queen, for without the land I am but a poor
princess. My mind is made up! I will sacrifice and perhaps lose
everything in order to save Bohemia, and you must direct all your
energy toward that end. All my soldiers, all of Hungary, will I lose
before I retreat even a step. The critical moment is finally upon us;
stop at nothing in order to succeed. Make certain that the troops are
happy and lack nothing; you know more about what is needed than
I do. Support my poor husband, who worries as much about the
men as about the land and who makes certain that they achieve all
that they are able to. Their condition fills him with sorrow, and what
the local people will not give them voluntarily, they must take by
force. You will say that I am cruel. That is true; but I also know that
for every cruelty I permit in order to save my land, I will compensate
one hundred fold. That I will do later, but for now I can only close
my heart with sorrow. I leave my fate to you; you know that I have
put my trust in you; I am very pleased that you have joined the
army. I flatter myself that all this effort will not be fruitless, and
that, since I have been singularly unfortunate until now, God will
finally grant me His favor. I am somewhat depressed, and everything
that concerns the present course of events worries me very much, in
fact too much for my present condition [at this moment Maria
Theresa was pregnant with her fifth child]. I regret the fate of all
those who suffer for my sake, and that is perhaps my greatest sorrow; but you will find in me at least an eternally grateful heart.

*Perhaps there exists no better example of Maria Theresa's
ability to inspire men to serve her than the following letter.
Accompanied by a portrait of herself and her infant son, it*

[2] Maria Theresa to Count Philip Kinsky, December, 1741, in Alfred von
Arneth, *Geschichte Maria Theresias* (Vienna: Wilhelm Braumüller, 1863) I, 346–
47. Translated by the editor.

*was sent to her new commander in chief Field Marshal Kheven-
hüller in January, 1742. Shortly after receiving it, Khevenhüller expelled the Bavarians from Austria, invaded Bavaria
itself, and on February 14 captured Munich, the capital city of
that land.*[3]

Beloved and loyal Khevenhüller:

Here you see before you a queen and her masculine inheritance
who have been abandoned by the whole world. What do you think
will become of this child? Look at this poor woman who must place
in your loyal hands, herself, her whole power, her authority, and
everything that our empire stands for and is capable of achieving.
Act, O hero and true vassal, as if you will have to justify yourself
before God and the world. Take righteousness as your shield; do
what you think is right; close your eyes to accusations of betrayal;
follow the undying deeds of your late teacher, Prince Eugene [Aus-
trian military hero from 1697 to 1736], and be confident that you
and your family will receive from our majesty and our successors
all grace, favor, and thanks now and forever, and from the world,
eternal admiration. Such we swear to you by our majesty.

Live long and strike hard!

*In 1756, eleven years after Austria and Prussia negotiated an
end to the War of the Austrian Succession, Maria Theresa and
Frederick the Great embarked on another struggle over Silesia,
this one known as the Seven Years' War. In the following letter,
written in mid-1758 to her chief foreign policy adviser, Count
Kaunitz, the empress again reveals her determination to continue the fight against her hated enemy despite Frederick's spec-
tacular victories at Rossbach (November 5, 1757) and Leuthen
(December 5, 1757). Especially notable in this passage are her
disgust with her French allies, who had retreated to defensive
positions behind the Rhine, and her resolution to again lock
her armies in combat to protect Bohemia and the city of
Prague.*[4]

You were right when you said that I would be unhappy with
the dispatches brought by the courier [from Paris]. I am most irri-

[3] Arneth, *Geschichte Maria Theresias*, II, 9. Translated by the editor.
[4] Arneth, *Geschichte Maria Theresias*, V, 523–26. Translated by the editor.

tated; our allies treat us like children. Instead of presenting the
facts forthrightly, they give us hopes and empty promises, and I am
certain that before April is over the [French] armies will fall back
across the Rhine because of supply shortages. They cannot say that
owing to the considerable losses of their magazines, insufficient provisions forced them to retreat across the Weser. They fell back because of bad planning and, I must add, their deficient will. Two
months ago we observed this failing determination in Paris but did
nothing about it. The French are excessive and unsteady in everything; even in the last campaign they thumbed their noses at the
enemy only while staying behind the Rhine, even though they had
nothing to fear from or even to do with him. The same thing has
happened again: they should deal honestly with us and not entice
us with projects and new ideas. But worst of all is their answer to
our memorandum concerning our operations; nothing seems more
wretched. While they are behind the Weser, they suggest we march
to the Elbe, even though they probably will not send us the 24,000
men they promised; meanwhile, the whole might of the king of
Prussia stands on our northern frontier and within a short time will
inundate first Bohemia and then perhaps Moravia. And they suggest
that we leave all our lands in order to occupy another in which
there exists no means of subsistence or good will, in which the smallest corps, the slightest movement by the king of Prussia will force us
to retreat, and in which we will lose our advantages and perhaps
our army by pursuing the same chimeras as last year. Indeed I cannot even think of it without losing my patience.

Why have we made the suggestion to advance to Schweidnitz? Not
to operate in Silesia, but to save that fortress, including the garrison
and artillery, which is so necessary to us and to have Schweidnitz in
front of us so we can better protect Bohemia and Moravia. We
cannot avoid battle if the king [of Prussia]—who commands a superior force—seeks it. But we will find it far more advantageous to
fight in Silesia than in Bohemia because, in case of victory, we can
completely change the situation to our advantage, and in case of
misfortune, we will run many fewer risks than in Bohemia. If the
king searches for battle in Bohemia, it has often been advised that
we avoid conflict, withdraw to defensible positions, and assume an
unaggressive posture. I know of no other strategy, but the example
the French offer us evokes no great desire to copy them. Their withdrawal is altogether shameful and amounts to a rout.

If the king of Prussia invades Bohemia, we must either fight or retreat as we have done until now. If we do the latter, we will lose all my lands and all their contributions for war as well as peace, and we must not deceive ourselves that a middle way exists. I am of the opinion that we must campaign as if there are no more Frenchmen, and we must not allow our own interests to be subverted on their behalf. [Field Marshal Leopold] Daun must have the authority to act as he thinks best and must be notified to expect nothing from the French army and to issue his orders accordingly. If we again abandon a part of Bohemia, we will lose not only our best source of manpower and provisions, but desertion will reach fearful proportions since two-thirds of the army consists of Bohemians. If Prague falls, all is lost, as we have experienced in previous campaigns. . . .

WEARINESS OF WAR

In the last years of Maria Theresa's reign war with Prussia again loomed on the horizon; this time, however, the chief Austrian protagonist was not the empress but her son and co-regent, Emperor Joseph II. Moreover, the focus of this confrontation centered on the Electorate of Bavaria, which, despite Frederick's protests Joseph wished to annex to the Habsburg state. By this time Maria Theresa had experienced years of Titanic struggle with the Prussian king without achieving her goal of retaking Silesia; at this point, she tried to convince her son of the futility of another war. Despite her age and past disappointments, she did not try to restrain him with emotional pleading; instead, she used logical arguments to show the military superiority of the Prussians and the relative diplomatic weakness of Austria. Whereas the bulk of the letter is in the handwriting of the empress's secretary, Charles Joseph Pichler, the last paragraph was written by the empress herself.[5]

The disadvantages and dangers evident from the moment we began our march into Bavaria were so obvious and so likely to worsen that I would be unworthy of being called sovereign and mother if I did not disregard my personal feelings and speak out.

Nothing less is at stake than the destruction of our house and monarchy and even the total disruption of all of Europe. No sacri-

[5] Maria Theresa to Joseph II, March 14, 1778, in Alfred von Arneth, ed., *Maria Theresia und Joseph II: Ihre Correspondenz* (Vienna: Carl Gerold's Sohn, 1867), II, 186–91. Translated by the editor.

fice is too great in order to prevent this catastrophe. I will happily risk all—accusations of speaking nonsense, of being weak, cowardly, even the degradation of my name—nothing will stop me from saving Europe from this dangerous situation. I know of no better way to employ the remainder of my unfortunate life. I vow that this decision costs me dearly, but it is done and I will stand by it. I must describe our military and political situation; I am obligated to do so because all that follows will be the consequence of this choice, which I owe to my conscience, my duty, and my love.

Compared to the king of Prussia, we have an army decidedly inferior by about thirty to forty thousand men, especially cavalry. He also has interior lines noticeably more advantageous, for we must ride twice as far to reach our required positions. He has fortresses, but we have none; we have vast areas to protect, and if we evacuate them, we expose them to invasion and insurrection. Such is the state of Galicia, where at most only 200 horse and 7 battalions of old invalids remain. It is an open country, newly conquered, and by no means secure. The spirit of freedom there is only dormant, and that nation has revealed that it is capable of revolt if someone just prods it a bit. No doubt the king of Prussia and, naturally, the king of Poland as well as his whole nation will not hesitate to take advantage of the first favorable opportunity to foment trouble as soon as we introduce the principle of might makes right—a principle from which no one has suffered more than we.

Hungary also has no troops, and directly across its frontier, Russia and Turkey will soon reignite their war. We know of the Prussian intrigues against us in Constantinople: the last letter from the king of Prussia to his representative there has revealed that nothing will be spared to bring into the war that enemy, who will be able to conquer all that he wishes in Hungary, since that land will be without men and fortresses. If our troops were in Saxony, even in Silesia (which I do not believe possible), or in the Upper Palatinate, we would be in no better position to defend these two great kingdoms of Galicia and Hungary. We would have to abandon them to their unhappy fate, at the mercy of a barbarous enemy and subject to all the ravages that will inevitably follow and which will ruin them for a century. I say nothing of our lands in Italy and the Low Countries or of our new possessions in Bavaria, all of which must be abandoned again.

Where will we find the resources to sustain this cruel war if at the outset we evacuate five countries of so much importance? What confidence, what credit will we establish in light of such measures in order to procure allies and monetary support? What will be our reputation in our own lands, when we pressure them in time of peace with taxes for defense, only to abandon them at the first sign of a war that, once begun, will end with their total ruin? Our destruction alone will save the remainder of Europe, and we will be guilty of causing it. This is what I can neither understand nor approve: it is total war.

Let us not delude ourselves; even if our armies prove successful, this success will amount to nothing. Two or three victorious battles will not gain for us a single county in Silesia, and it will require many campaigns and even years before the struggle will end. We have the example of 1757 to convince us that our enemy will not yield easily. The task of just conducting a war takes time to develop, so we will have to fight for at least three or four years, even if we do well. This length of time will allow all of Europe to intervene in the struggle in order to prevent our becoming too powerful, especially since everyone mistrusts us so much even now. In these circumstances I cannot think of a single friend or ally upon whom we could depend with assurance. We must compare our resources not only vis-à-vis those of the king of Prussia but vis-à-vis all those who oppose our aggrandizement, and that includes all of Europe. How can we hope to defy all of them? Time is against us. The longer the war drags on, the more new enemies we will have to fight. At the beginning of the struggle, it will by no means be militarily advisable for us to risk a decisive battle; it will be necessary for us to try to win time in order to bewilder the king and to increase our army little by little, albeit the reinforcements will consist by more than a third of young, inexperienced recruits. But even this interval, useful for operations, will turn in another way to our disadvantage. While we hold the king in check, his superior light troops will ravage our provinces and destroy our resources. In the meantime our neighbors, encouraged by the intrigues of the king and motivated by the same reasons that inspired us to invade Poland and Bavaria, will do the same to our other possessions. All in all, we have nothing to gain and everything to lose. All of our troops will be united at one location; if we are defeated there, nothing will remain.

It will be unfortunate if this picture I have drawn, albeit very true, comes to the attention of others, even our most loyal subjects, but I will spare nothing in order to find some means of preventing this debacle. Once the sword is drawn, no time for conciliation will remain. The welfare of thousands and thousands of men, the existence of the monarchy, and the preservation of our house depend upon it. After all I have said, I must emphasize to you that I cannot act contrary to my conscience and convictions; this is neither whimsy nor personal timidity. I have the same courage as I had thirty years ago, but I cannot permit the destruction of my house and my state. (If the war erupts, do not depend on me. I am going to retire to the Tyrol, finish my days there in luxurious retreat, occupy myself only with tears for the misfortunes of my house and my people, and try to end my unhappy life as a good Christian.)

I have read the two letters to the emperor and to Kaunitz; I have again emphasized that both believe I am wrong, that I exaggerate. I hope that I have worried too much; when all is said and done, perhaps I will no longer be alive. This last, inserted passage I have added later; they have not seen it.

HATRED OF FREDERICK OF PRUSSIA

Throughout her reign Maria Theresa considered Frederick the Great the archvillain of Europe. In this passage, a portion of a letter written on June 20, 1778, as part of her efforts to dissuade Joseph from continuing his conflict with Prussia, the empress reveals her hatred of the "Monster" Frederick.[6]

I had the same opinion as you that this villainous king has stooped so low as to approach Kaunitz, from whom he thinks he can obtain a better arrangement than from you. There you see what this great man, whom everyone calls a Solomon, is really like. By observing him closely and constantly, one can see that he is very petty and a veritable charlatan, concealed only by his power and good luck. I do not want to appear too proud, but my Joseph is not like him at all and works much differently as well. The best testimony is the way the army is managed and provisioned, the dispatches to Cobenzl and to me, and finally the letters between you and this Monster, which I reread frequently to receive new inspira-

[6] Maria Theresa to Joseph II, June 20, 1778, in Arneth, *Maria Theresia und Joseph II*, II, 298–99. Translated by the editor.

tion. I am in need of such reviving because I am depressed, and I inform you that the last memorandum of the king of Prussia via Cobenzl appears to me quite appropriate. Unfortunately, we are in the wrong and do not speak plainly—indeed we cannot—because we want unjust gains. We hope by the course of events to seize them outright, or offer Lusatia to the king of Prussia as a decoy. I have often said that this time it is not possible to relent and follow a course iniquitous to our principles without exposing ourselves completely. Events have gone too far, and this response will bring a war that God may or may not render less bloody and shorter than its predecessors. Those are my thoughts for now; I send them to you such as they are and embrace you tenderly but sadly. Adieu.

2
Reforms

The most far-reaching consequences of Maria Theresa's reign lay in her numerous reforms. They were implemented during two separate periods, the first and more important lasting from 1746 to 1756 and the second stretching from 1761 to 1778. Undoubtedly the reforms of the first period were aimed at strengthening the state—improving finances, enlarging the army, and streamlining the administration—they were not concerned with altering the fabric of society. Maria Theresa wished to subordinate many of the empire's human and material resources to the central government so that it could more effectively wage war to maintain the possessions of the House of Habsburg. In the second period, when war ceased to be Maria Theresa's foremost concern, the reforms reflected an increasing desire to upgrade the economic and civil condition of her subjects. Although built largely upon the earlier changes, in many cases they forecast the wholesale innovations to be introduced by Joseph after the empress's death. By and large the reforms of both periods were introduced only in the so-called German lands of the empire (the Austrian and Bohemian provinces) and not in the Hungarian, Italian, or Belgian territories.

THE NEED

In her Political Testament, *Maria Theresa emphatically expressed the need for reform, especially at the administrative level. In her opinion the major culprits of the bureaucracy were the chief ministers of the chancellories. Each crownland possessed an Estate, a body composed of the leading aristocrats, clergymen, and townspeople of the province, which each year voted a certain sum of money for the sovereign's use. The official primarily in charge of negotiating with the Estate was the head of the chancellory under whose jurisdiction the crownland fell. By utilizing his office as middleman between Estate and crown, this minister—who was usually a great landowner himself—could extract favors from both. On the one*

30

hand, he could try to keep the Estate's contributions as low as possible, and on the other hand, he could assure the ruler a certain sum when it was needed. In this passage Maria Theresa complains of this practice, blames her ancestors for their failure to restrict it, and expresses her reasons for reforming the whole financial and administrative system to abolish it.[1]

Here I will mention briefly a few thoughts about my predecessors. Out of feelings of great piety they gave away many—actually most—of the crown estates and income, which at that time served to finance the spread of religion and to improve the clergy. But since God has blessed us now in the German lands with a flourishing Catholic faith and a well-endowed priesthood, this need is no longer pressing. In fact, not only do I consider it unworthy, but actually criminal to give the clergy more funds because, on the one hand, they do not need it, and on the other, they unfortunately do not use what they have to good advantage and thereby do a disservice to the people. No cloister observes the rules of its order and many idlers are admitted. All this will require a thorough reform when, after proper preparation, I have the time to implement it.

Of course I exempt the kingdom of Hungary from these measures because there much good can still be achieved in religious matters. In this effort I shall demand the cooperation of the priests, but not them exclusively, for I plan to work primarily with laymen to carry out certain changes, particularly the creation of seminaries, colleges, academies, hospitals for the sick and wounded, and conservatories for unwed mothers—as exist in Italy—and for the educational betterment of the youth. All must be undertaken carefully with the thought of creating and expanding that which serves the general public and not merely the interests of the clergy, monasteries, or convents in each province. But it must be understood that not even this noble purpose can succeed completely until the military can be adequately strengthened to protect the monarchy and the welfare of its provinces and people.

I must also mention the crown revenues, which pay for the expenses of the court and the diplomatic service, and the state debt, upon which rests the preservation of the monarchy and without

[1] Alfred von Arneth, ed., "Zwei Denkschriften der Kaiserin Maria Theresia," *Archiv für österreichische Geschichte*, XLVII (1871), 294–304. Translated by the editor.

which no state can survive. When these financial requirements are met, a ruler must turn his attention to the relief of his lands and subjects, especially the poor among them, and by no means must he divert his revenue to indulge in amusement, ceremony, or magnificence.

Although I may not live to experience such a blissful time, I hope through my tireless exertion, care, and toil to put things in such a condition that, God willing, in fifty years—and perhaps sooner— some beneficial results will be forthcoming. Confidently will I rely upon my descendants to continue these reforms in the spirit of virtue, piety, and justice, as well as fatherly love, generosity, and concern for their lands and subjects—all of which they learned in their youth. Should this not occur, God forbid, then I wish and in fact beg God that if foreign rulers or even the enemy himself would more capably serve and protect our lands, then it would be a thousand times better that they should govern them.

But to return once again to my ancestors, these individuals not only gave away most of the crown estates, but absorbed also the debts of those properties confiscated in time of rebellion, and these debts are still in arrears. Emperor Leopold [Maria Theresa's grandfather, who ruled from 1658 to 1705] found little left to give away, but the terrible wars he fought no doubt forced him to mortgage or pawn additional crown estates. His successors did not relieve these burdens, and when I became sovereign, the crown revenues barely reached eighty thousand gulden. Also in the time of my forebears, the ministers received enormous payments from the crown and from the local Estates because they knew not only how to exploit selfishly the good will, grace, and munificence of the Austrian house by convincing each ruler that his predecessor had won fame by giving freely but also how to win the ears of the provincial lords and clergy so that these ministers acquired all that they wished. In fact they spread their influence so wide that in the provinces they were more feared and respected than the ruler himself. And when they had finally taken everything from the sovereign, these same ministers turned for additional compensation to their provinces, where their great authority continuously increased. Even though complaints reached the monarch, out of grace and forebearance toward the ministers, he simply allowed the exploitation to continue.

Although the opportunities to make great profits had largely disappeared by the reigns of Joseph [Maria Theresa's uncle, who ruled from 1705 to 1711] and Charles, the ministers still made use of every chance to enrich themselves or their relatives through gifts and promotions.

None of the emperors could undermine the prestige or power of the ministers because each served in effect as the sovereign in his own department.

Generally such ministers used the Estates as they wished in all the lands because they were, by and large, the wealthiest landowners in the provinces and therefore enjoyed the greatest prestige and influence. In fact, many received large annual remunerations from the Estates themselves. If a ruler wished to procure a set payment from the provinces for the maintenance of his army and the salvation of the whole monarchy, he had to pay to these same ministers, who alone could grant him what he wished, any grace or favor they demanded.

This system gave the ministers such authority that the sovereign himself found it convenient for his own interests to support them because he learned by experience that the more prestige enjoyed by the heads of the provinces, the more of the sovereign's demands these heads could extract from their Estates.

The natural mildness and grace of the Austrian house, which did not permit the removal of anyone from office unless he had proven himself totally unworthy, encouraged many of these ministers to openly oppose the monarch and his interests in the Estates, and even to flatter themselves into thinking that they were not merely ministers, as at other courts, but coregents or at least autonomous authorities.

Emperor Leopold was the only one of my ancestors who kept a firm grip on his sovereign authority and who intended to maintain it against everyone, even by changing ministers frequently and, under special circumstances, disgracing them. Nonetheless, these efforts only made the ministers more cautious, and he did not try to abolish the old constitution, which alone could have removed these abuses.

Should a ministry change hands, the successor usually had not the same prejudices as the former minister, but was so determined to maintain the traditional principles of defending his authority and enjoying the advantages of his position that often such a change only made the malfeasance worse. I myself have experienced some changes of officers that appeared neither to augment my authority nor to reduce the previous corruption.

These abuses have sprung from two major causes. The first consists of that self-interest and desire to dominate found in most people but especially in those ministers who are so wealthy in the provinces. Even should these posts change hands, the new men followed in the same path, reflecting more concern for their own welfare and that of their relatives than for the good of the community.

As to the other cause, these ministers and leaders of the crownlands represented to the monarch such an accumulation of privileges and liberties that the general welfare was simply overlooked. In order to procure from the Estates that which was necessary in an emergency, the sovereign had to pander to the interests and prestige of his ministers, even to grant favors willingly in order to salvage the state from its threatened demise.

When examined closely, these pretentious customs are based primarily on practical and mutually advantageous privileges granted to the Estates by earlier monarchs. Although originally the common property of the general Estates, these customs, in view of their periodic reconfirmation, have contributed to the prestige, credit, and powers of the ministers. But because the words "honorable privileges" exist in the confirmations, the monarch need only honor the good, and not the bad, practices that have developed since.

It is certain that in no state would the Estates have won such broad freedoms had they not received such powerful support from the ministers, whose authority and prestige in turn depended solely on what they did for the Estates. Blame for such conditions rests primarily on the ruler because, in order to obtain quick and easy money, he willingly gave away or granted anything. All things considered, if the sovereign had not been dependent on the arbitrary decisions of the Estates to fulfill his requests, he would not have found it necessary to turn to the influence and reputations of the ministers to satisfy his needs.

This is the real reason why under my ancestors the power and prestige of the ministers rose so high and, to the detriment of the monarchical authority, exceeded all reasonable limits, and why, as long as the old constitution persisted, a monarch was ill-advised to encroach upon or diminish their authority.

These ministers have used their inside influence with the monarch to promote the interests of the province they ruled and in which they owned property. Consequently, the other crownlands suffered and at times were viewed as if they were foreign lands, not belonging to the same lord.

This was the outstanding reason why, as soon as I realized it, I undertook ever-widening reforms to carry out a complete change in the government.

The pervasive jealousy, ill will, and slander among these ministers led to the most injurious animosities and irreparable prejudices, which have undermined the most worthy measures and have colored official advice with such innumerable, egotistical biases that the monarch has often experienced acute embarrassment.

Whereas many of my predecessors have been accused of laxity and indecisiveness in provincial and governmental affairs, the real reason for their vacillation lay in the ministers' unending disharmony and each one's selfish defense of his point of view, all of which quite naturally made the sovereign indecisive because he feared that his own opinion was incorrect.

This persistent disunity among the ministers under all the emperors has often placed land and people in the greatest danger of collapse, out of which only providential concern has salvaged and preserved this house.

After Ferdinand [emperor from 1619 to 1637] crushed the Bohemian rebellion, he overwhelmed his loyal ministers and servants with gifts and favors, but these men used their influence, acquired in the newly instituted Bohemian constitution, more for the benefit of the land than for the interests of the prince, even though the land had been subdued by force of arms.

Regarding the Bohemian provinces, the office of supreme chancellor for Bohemia brought with it the greatest inconvenience to the emperor and the most unfortunate results. Without the agreement of the supreme chancellor, the sovereign could hardly implement anything he had personally decided on or had concluded upon the advice of his other ministers. From this very abuse emerged the natural result that the whole chancellory showed itself much more willing to follow an order from its supreme chancellor than one issued by the monarch, so that the power of the supreme chancellor appeared virtually unassailable, a situation completely incompatible with royal authority and service.

This was simply the outcome of the indulgence and grace shown by my ancestors toward the great and mighty in these lands, even though this same mildness and grace had provided these people with their exalted positions. At the same time some families have utilized their acquired offices to make certain that if one of their number is eligible, that office reverts to him, causing these enormous powers to pass from father to son. Therefore, the complete elimination of this

office of supreme chancellor is quite necessary for the improvement
of the bureaucracy. It cannot be denied that the Bohemian chancellory observed much better order in its affairs than the Austrian
chancellory and did not lightly permit any encroachment upon its
authority by the Estates; however, it had no misgivings about hiding
from its sovereign information about the inner workings of the administration and seeing to it that the monarch remained quite un-
informed. This veil was designed to prevent the central treasury
from interfering in provincial affairs. Such conditions made it impossible to secure respect for and implementation of royal opinions
and decrees without the approval of the chancellory. Therefore the
supreme chancellor had the opportunity to strengthen more and
more his influence and power and often to use it to the disadvantage
of the other crownlands; when their influence became greater than
that of the Bohemian chancellor, the ministers of these other crownlands reacted in kind, to the detriment of Bohemia.

And since the government usually consisted of more Austrian
officials than Bohemians, the former have, for the most part, pre-
dominated over the latter.

These existing conditions have given rise to such a deep-rooted
and unmitigated hatred among the crownlands that each official in
the administrations—down to the lowest bureaucrat and adviser—
has painstakingly employed every lawful device to undermine the
others. The Austrian contingent has outdone all the others and has
also exceeded all in its pretentions.

This animosity the Hungarians especially have experienced, since
the others sought to keep them in permanent subjugation and to
prevent any of them from holding office. The apparent pretext for
such oppression was the unrest and rebellion in Hungary which persisted until the time of Charles VI. But reasonableness and practical
politics demand that the wheat be separated from the chaff and
that those who deserve favor not be condemned along with the unworthy lest they sink into dejection and desperation.

Thus the evidence shows how the ministers of my predecessors in
no way followed a policy designed to improve the service, but only
used their acquired power to promote their own interests, distribute
offices to their family and friends, and generally to follow the old,
deep-rooted practices of their ancestors.

It is a wonder that my forebears would even consent to entrust
the maintenance of the monarchy to such men.

To prove my point further, we only need to consider the conditions of the Austrian lands upon my succession. These states have governed themselves as they pleased with little or no interference from the chancellory, and the state documents and provincial accounts indicate that even the slightest threats of investigation were artfully diverted by generous bribes and gifts, of which the monarch himself was frequently a recipient.

The primary evil was that at that time the ministers looked after their own provinces only, and none was willing to assume any general responsibility. Consequently, the general calamities in the Italian [part of War of the Polish Succession] and Hungarian [war with the Turks] wars became worse because each minister dared not demand additional sacrifices from the land in his trust and contented himself with criticizing others at every opportunity. These conditions limited the amount of credit available in each province, and yet such credit was necessary to support the needs of the state. Since no general funds or treasury income existed to provide collateral, all funds had to be collected on the credit of the provincial war tax, which provided no relief to the monarch or the taxpayer but provided great profits for a few. The long-lasting peace [1718–1733] served as a time only to confuse the sovereign, to increase the factions, and to find a way of implementing the ridiculous Spanish plans, which a number of ministers favored and even the monarch viewed with some sympathy.

Therefore, at the outbreak of the war, everything was in the greatest confusion, without any system or plan in internal or foreign affairs, and the monarchy was plunged into the greatest danger. At that time the domestic debt of the Austrian provinces exceeded 24 million [gulden], whose interest alone reached 1.2 million which had to be paid from the military revenues. The result was all the more reprehensible because in order to exempt the great landowners, who by and large paid absolutely nothing, the provinces had paid their earlier taxes with borrowed capital.

These difficult conditions prompted me to judge the suggestions of my ministers and advisers with more caution.

Yet my conscientiousness reaped no benefits until I finally realized that I must reform the whole internal constitution.

To the detriment of my service, the disharmony was so great within the entire bureaucracy that I, like my predecessors, found it necessary to spend most of my time quelling these damaging disputes. The ministers directed their greatest bitterness toward the central treasury, and almost all the ministers, even the most antagonistic, united in sabotaging this office.

The treasury itself was lifeless, abandoned on all sides. Although its purpose was to collect money, the chancellories deflected every attempt it made to do so. The overwhelming debt of the state and the excessive confusion within the treasury, which persisted owing to some plotted corruption, led to various inequities, which all the ministers and the public protested. Nonetheless, no ministry had the means or the will to rectify the financial situation, and it appeared that the incessant struggle among the bureaus would have continued until the fall of the monarchy had I not decided to pluck this evil out by its roots.

FINANCES

In the earlier reform period, Maria Theresa's first thought was to create a large and effective standing army. Accepting from her military advisers an estimate that a standing force of 110,000 would best serve the needs of the state, she set out to change the financial structure in order to procure the revenues necessary to maintain an army of that size. To create the new system, Maria Theresa chose the brilliant and incorruptible Count Frederick William Haugwitz, who composed a plan to secure the needed funds. According to his proposal, the Estates, which provided the bulk of the funds for military expenditures, would not agree to a contribution each year as they had in the past; instead a sum, which would be paid in monthly installments, would be set for ten years. Such a system would enable the government to predict a certain annual revenue and to project its expenditures accordingly. To reward the Estates for their approval of this plan, Haugwitz suggested the abolition of all their obligations to provision and house soldiers stationed in their provinces. In this passage from her Political Testament, *Maria Theresa relates how she supported Haugwitz, over the objections of the other ministers, in the implementation of his plan.*[2]

In another section, I have already explained the defects and misuses of the internal constitution. I became increasingly inclined

[2] Arneth, ed., "Zwei Denkschriften Maria Theresias," 308–15. Translated by the editor.

to abolish this [constitution] because, as Divine Providence revealed, as it then stood it was impossible to implement the measures necessary for the maintenance of the monarchy.

Each of my ministers admitted that to maintain the more than 100,000 men needed to protect crown and sceptre, we would have to reorder our financial system, which had fallen into severe confusion.

To achieve this purpose, I instructed my ministers to compose their thoughts on the subject in writing, and to work out such a system at the earliest possible moment. I observed, however, that despite my frequent memoranda, no ideas appeared, and it seemed that my ministers were more inclined toward argument and debate than in dealing with the urgent problem at hand. In any case, the work dragged on and on, and no one appeared willing or able to tackle it earnestly. At this time, good fortune and the grace of God introduced me to Count Haugwitz, who, out of loyalty and devotion, had left all his possessions in Silesia in order to suffer through the difficult times here with me. I first began to know him through His Majesty the Emperor and later through Count [Emmanuel] Silva Tarouca, who was my counselor in matters concerning Italy and the Netherlands and in all my personal affairs as well. During those first, difficult years, I received much good advice and encouragement from him. He helped me become thoroughly acquainted with people and the affairs of state, but he never personally intervened in provincial or national matters, preferring that I act according to my own inclinations so that he could make me aware of my mistakes. This is most important for a ruler, and men willing to follow such a course are hard to find since most act out of self-respect or personal interest. I wish that all my children will find someone just like him, who will take them by the hand in similar circumstances. I owe Tarouca much, and I will take great pains to acknowledge to his children my debt to him, and my successors will do the same.

To return to Haugwitz, truly he was sent by Divine Providence because, in order to break through these delays, I needed such a man —honorable, without personal design, predilections, ambitions, or favorites. He supported what was good because he recognized it as good, and he revealed a magnanimous disinterestedness and attachment to his monarch, without prejudices, but with great ability, love of work, and steady application, not dreading exposure nor the unreasonable hatred directed at him by private interests. In fact, even Count Harrach, his greatest opponent—as I will illustrate later—

confided to me many times that without Haugwitz the reforms could never have been effected and that I needed such a man for this job. I could trust only him to undertake these changes, and in everything the mighty hand of God protected him.

In this extremely difficult situation that I have already described, with the emperor's approval I authorized Haugwitz by way of the cabinet secretary, [Ignatius] Koch, to compose a plan for the maintenance of 110,000 men, to be supported with the greatest possible economy. The plan should provide for the abolition of all military excesses and the greatest relief possible for the crownlands. Haugwitz's recommendations, which the emperor and I approved completely, laid on the one hand the foundation for the peace and quiet of the provinces through relief from all military oppression and, on the other, the maximum economy, but with provision for all necessary expenditure.

I allowed Count Haugwitz to reveal his plan confidentially to the supreme chancellor, Count Harrach [Harrach replaced Kinsky as supreme chancellor of Bohemia in 1745]. The chancellor revealed that he completely agreed with the main points, as did all the ministers, although a few declared that they should examine exactly the ability of the provinces to pay the requested sums. This reasonable opposition was easily put to rest by composing daily balance sheets which showed that when all the taxes, contributions, and other debts of the state and private persons were calculated together, the final totals invariably exceeded the demands of the new system, thus winning for it many supporters.

The first major problem inflicted upon this reform involved the division of the sums among the various crownlands. Some ministers appealed to an imaginary traditional appropriation; with it they tried to impose an exorbitant assessment upon the Inner Austrian lands [Styria, Carinthia, and Carniola], the poorest and most burdened of all. The chief proponent of this suggestion, Count Harrach, also proposed that all indirect taxes and sales taxes in the provinces be abolished—millions would be lost—and that the Estates be responsible for paying any portion of the maintenance of the 110,000 men and the interest on the state debt that the remaining crown properties could not cover. I found no one approving this.

Some believed Harrach's plan completely unfeasible and argued that the Bank of Vienna would collapse (an event I will always try to prevent) if we compelled the provinces to pay the 27 million in additional taxes that Harrach's plan would necessitate, especially since abolition of the sales tax would make the direct taxes almost impossible for the taxpayers to bear. Furthermore, neither I nor my ministers could assume the responsibility for allowing these taxes, which my forebears had levied and collected, to slip from our control, thus returning the whole essence of the monarchy—its income and complete financial welfare—to the capricious and arbitrary disposition of the Estates. Such an act would greatly reduce the monarchical authority; it would benefit provincial or a few private interests but in the long run would by no means serve the general welfare. As I have used my authority because I believed it necessary and healthy for the state, so would I gladly and quickly reduce it if I believed that justice and reasonableness for all would be better served through the administration of the Estates. In this case, however, I am convinced the opposite result would develop, and I see that the lords or ministers were seeking their own advantage by trying to pit the monarch against the Estates in order to win favors from both. Consequently, I could never agree to such a concept.

Count Harrach's project did propose wide-sweeping commercial reforms in order to make it possible for the taxpayers to pay these exorbitant sums; they would require ten years to implement, however, and thus cancel any hopes for immediate relief for the taxpayers.

Shortly thereafter Count Harrach's project suffered defeat by a unanimous vote in council, which I had noted in a special record book. Because no one could suggest anything different or better than Haugwitz's systematic project, which, in private discussions with Bartenstein, I had already approved anyway, I decided to send Count Haugwitz to Moravia and Bohemia to inquire of the Estates there as to what degree they would be inclined to approve these ideas as being in their own best interest.

The ministers, especially the supreme chancellor, Count Harrach, predicted and, in fact, convinced themselves that the Estates would never approve such a project. Instead of voicing a few critical remarks, however, they tried hard to sabotage good relations among the Estates. This effort was all the more dangerous because they also misrepresented Haugwitz's project to the Estates.

But just as I had relied upon Divine Providence to maintain the monarchy, so I became aware of continued Divine Assistance when Count Haugwitz overcame all the obstacles the ministers set before him and secured the consent of the Moravian Estates for the permanent military system and all of its ramifications. I ordered him to present the same proposals in Bohemia. Here Haugwitz encountered a few more obstacles, caused largely by the misconceptions fomented by the gossipy and intriguing interests in Vienna.

Despite this trouble, the project was approved in Bohemia as well, and at the close of the sessions, the deputies to the Estates in Bohemia and Moravia came to Vienna. Count Harrach and a few other ministers maintained that the Estates in both lands had been rushed—indeed, bribed—into accepting Haugwitz's proposals (in no province have I given or promised the least favor, and no one has asked for any), and Harrach added that they at least should have requested certain conditions that he recommended.

At this time I personally asked the assembled delegates of both lands if they believed Harrach's idea practicable. Unanimously they replied that his plan was unfeasible and in fact seemed a mirage that could neither be put into effect nor could last. They also agreed that the advantages promised by Harrach were only speculative in nature, founded on no solid facts.

But Count Haugwitz did agree with the supreme chancellor and the other ministers in one respect; namely, that this new military system would provide no strengthening of the monarchy unless there were corresponding reforms in the state debt and treasury.

Even Count Harrach knew that the cameral funds were insufficient for these two purposes because he himself had computed the needs of the treasury and the debt.

I still could not accept Harrach's ideas, however, because they would have deprived the Bank of Vienna of most of its funds and thereby would have ruined it. Furthermore, everyone agreed that the suppositions upon which his plans were based did not, and never would, exist.

Consequently, I felt obliged to allow Count Haugwitz to compose a system for the debt and treasury, which, despite the boundless chaos in both offices, finally went into effect. The plan concluded that, after providing for normal expenditures, payment of the interest on the debt at 6 percent—rather 5 percent on the interest and 1 percent on the balance—and the continuation of the Bank of Vienna's privileges, a deficit of approximately 2,500,000 would remain. To secure this sum in order to stabilize the overall system, I had to ask for contributions from the Estates, and, since the Bohemian and Moravian delegates still remained in Vienna, I personally prepared a speech, explaining to them exactly what was needed. They were impressed by my request and promised to personally support my suggestions among their fellow delegates. Through their influence, the Estates of Bohemia, Moravia, and Silesia promised the funds to overcome the shortage.

In Lower Austria the established land marshal was Count Harrach. Because he refused to influence those Estates to accept the two million in taxes assigned to them, I had to appoint Count Haugwitz commissioner and Count [Charles Adam] Bräuner land marshal to replace Harrach. These changes proved effective, for the Lower Austrian Estates willingly accepted the two million and, like the Bohemian delegates, agreed to a ten-year recess.

In Upper Austria, where I could not send Haugwitz, the Estates appeared much more reluctant to accept the one million assigned to them. At the end of their sessions, however, the deputies finally agreed, and everything came out all right.

The greatest difficulties developed in the three Inner Austrian lands. In all of the Austrian provinces, but especially there, finances were run in such an unbusinesslike and irresponsible manner that the courts, as the chancellories used to be called, allowed them to accumulate a so-called domestic debt of 24,000,000 whose interest alone reached 1,200,000 annually. The debt of these lands made their treasury payments so high that the allotment assigned to Inner Austria was considered unbearable, and it was true that certain localities would be unable to pay it.

Before my reign, these Inner Austrian lands received special privileges, frequently avoiding the payment of their required assessments by promising to pay in the future. Consequently, the introduction of systematic tax collection fell upon them much harder than on the others. Styria, for instance, only with some difficulty, could accept a recess of just three years.

In Carniola a whole year was needed before they could agree to a three years' recess, and even then only after we remitted their debt.

In Carinthia we could do nothing because the Estates rejected all reasonable suggestions, and I found myself obliged to collect the quota by using my rights as sovereign. I had, the year before, instructed Count Haugwitz to send two commissioners to help them; the Estates acknowledged their acceptance to one of the commissioners, Count Rudolph Chotek, but reneged three weeks later, complaining that they could not afford the cost. Concurrently, however, they refused to lower their provincial or administrative funds and even suggested—out of ignorance or villainy—to tax the serfs even more. For this reason I chose to collect the taxes myself.

The continuous laments of the Estates that they could not meet their requirements because of their own debts and poor business methods convinced me to institute a better and more equitable management of local finances. I must emphasize that the Estates, by abusing their excessive freedoms, carry the primary responsibility for the deterioration of my crownlands. In general, the Estates ignored what was just; most of their leaders followed the examples of their predecessors, concerning themselves only with private interests, denying all reasonable requests from the poor and oppressed, and allowing the Estates to persecute each other.

ADMINISTRATION

Two major administrative reforms were introduced in the early reform period. The first involved the abolition of the Austrian and Bohemian chancellories, whose rivalry had caused so much trouble, and the assignment of their responsibilities to a single administrative and financial bureau known as the Directorium in Publicus et Cameralibus (General Directory), *under the presidency of the versatile Count Haugwitz. The second major change called for the transfer of all judicial matters from the chancellories to the Supreme Judiciary, which served as both the ministry of justice and supreme court. Although Maria Theresa at first regarded the creation of the General Directory as her most important innovation, during the second reform period she altered its character by dividing the financial and administrative functions into separate ministries.*[3]

In order to build my reforms into a stable and durable regime, I knew that I must depart from the old traditional, but faulty, constitution and enact measures necessary to conform with my newly instituted system.

To make these changes permanent, I decided that, in order to direct and authorize the appropriate resolutions personally, His Majesty the Emperor and I would attend the weekly sessions designed to create the new administration. To prepare the material regarding these reforms, I established a commission under the presidency of Count Haugwitz which included one representative each

---

[3] Arneth, ed., "Zwei Denkschriften Maria Theresias," 320–24. Translated by the editor.

from the Bohemian and Austrian chancellories, a treasury official, and an officer from the general war commissariat. In the provinces I established in each city a deputation whose sole duty was to collect and classify all material relating to the system, whether it concerned the treasury or the military.

Soon I realized that my major goals could not be reached quite yet because both chancellories and the treasury—in fact, almost all the ministers—vigorously opposed this new institution. They realized that it would reduce their authority and influence, and hoped to find, either in the short or long run, opportunities to dilute or sabotage it in order to restore things to their old footing. Likewise, the lower officials in the ministries, who should have welcomed these reforms, opposed them most strongly, threatened to undermine them openly, and through their comments caused the people to have the wrong impression of them. And because I wished to stabilize the whole system not just for the present, but also for the future so that my children would not fall into the labyrinth that I have, I undertook some reforms with too much haste and on too grand a scale and thereby alienated many people, especially those with much influence. Furthermore, owing to limited revenues, I could grant no help or relief to the poor and oppressed, and their protests caused me much additional unpopularity.

After considerable thought I concluded that the foremost evil affecting my monarchy was that each minister and bureaucrat constantly played the advocate and protector of the province entrusted to him and dealt only lukewarmly with matters concerning the general welfare of the monarchy. They endeavored to transfer unjustly their responsibilities to other provinces and to discredit the central treasury, which as a result proved ineffective in serving the requirements of the administation or the general will. The treasury was reduced to keeping the books and juggling figures. In an emergency, however, these same ministers expected the treasury to come up with the money to meet all contingencies, even though they knew it was empty-handed and its resources limited. Furthermore, instead of advancing general policy in an atmosphere of understanding, the ministers wasted time in the most unnecessary and damaging manner by engaging in arguments and irrelevancies and ignoring the question at hand. Consequently, we almost always missed the best opportunity to institute a new measure. I therefore resolved to change the pernicious constitution both at the center and in the provinces and thereby stabilize our systematic reforms.

To achieve this end I removed all the offices of the Austrian and Bohemian chancellories and preserved only those dealing with Hungary and the household treasury, allowing the latter to survive only so long as its president lived [Count John Francis Gottfried Dietrichstein, who died in 1755]. I abolished both chancellories and transferred all public, financial, and nontechnical military affairs to the newly created General Directory.

Shortly thereafter, I established a Supreme Judiciary to insure effective justice in both the Austrian and Bohemian crownlands (this court also collected the employment lists, decisions, and departments of the Austrian and Bohemian courts). My purpose here was to cement further the uniformity in all the government bureaus and to make certain that no one had the opportunity to appeal on any grounds to the old, prejudicial constitution.

To assist in this reform, I abolished the old title of chancellor and called the heads and assistant heads of the General Directory and the Supreme Judiciary "presidents." In the provinces I established everywhere "representations" to care for public, financial, and nontechnical military business. To these representations were attached the already established war commissariats in order to make their business easier and more uniform. Just as the business of the provincial representations fell under the purview of the General Directory, so the provincial courts had to file their reports to the Supreme Court, which in turn had the authority to intervene in the processes and verdicts of all trials without waiting for my approval.

On the other hand, all resolutions approved by the General Directory must be sent to me weekly, and on each Friday it must meet in the presence of the emperor and myself to discuss the more important matters. Generally I have insisted that all business be concluded each week and nothing be postponed, except that which requires a more thorough preparation.

For commercial affairs I have created another directory which consists mostly of administrators attached to the General Directory and which must work closely with it in all matters. The president of the commercial directory attends a session of the General Directory weekly and joins me at the conference on internal affairs.

I am convinced that these reforms will provide the solid foundation for this monarchy, which, with God's continued help, I will preserve for the benefit and use of my successors. These changes will give the monarch the opportunity to possess a true knowledge of the disposition of his lands, to discuss and examine their complaints, to insure a rightful, acceptable balance between upper and lower classes, and to be especially watchful that the rich and powerful do not oppress the poor and lowly.

Because the new system restricts the previously excessive authority of the ministers and bureaucrats, it is easy to assume that the majority of them will consider these measures unbearable and will only slowly appreciate their benefits. In the meantime, they will try to poison the public through misleading and impassioned speeches, which probably should be stopped. Believing, however, that these criticisms will slowly cease and the people will realize that these reforms will be for the best, I have largely ignored or scorned these speeches. Nonetheless, because these arguments have noticeably had a very bad influence on the public and might actually do substantial harm, I may have to place some restraint on them.

ARMY

To improve the army's ability to fight constituted the goal of Maria Theresa's financial and administrative reforms, and, by the early 1750s, the army was indeed far more effective than the force of ten years earlier. In the following passage, taken from her second Political Testament, *an edited, less repetitious, but more impersonal revision of the first, Maria Theresa describes the improvements introduced in the military. The reader should particularly note three innovations: the punctual payment of wages, the establishment of military academies for young officers—none existed prior to her reign—and the reform of the* Grenzers, *Slavic peoples who formed military colonies on the empire's southeastern border to protect the Habsburg lands from Turkish raids.*[4]

Never was the army stronger than from 1720 to 1734, and no one would have thought to deny that my father's reign was enlightened and intelligent. Without mentioning the foreign lands under his rule like Naples and Sicily—which still contributed a few millions yearly to the enrichment of the public—the crownlands consisted then of all the same lands as today, plus all of Silesia, Glatz, Wallachia, Serbia, and a portion of the Banat of Timişoara. At that time the treasury had to support no more than 60,000 regu-

[4] Arneth, ed., "Zwei Denkschriften Maria Theresias," 349–52. Translated by the editor.

lars in peacetime, in addition to a much smaller number of irregulars in both generalities in Serbia, on the Sava River, and on the
Tisza and Maros rivers; although only a small part of these forces
could be used outside their native land, they cost much less at that
time. Regarding the barracks in Hungary and the German crownlands, the regulars certainly lived richly, as did the noncommissioned officers in the fortresses, who enjoyed certain compensations
that made up in other ways for their meager pay and infrequent
leaves. They also worried less when each year they received no pay
throughout the summer. Responsibility for this lack of payment lay
upon poor finances; nothing was taken off the balance of the state
debt, so the court, administrative, and foreign service expenses remained partially unpaid.

In spite of the loss of Silesia, Glatz, and the provinces surrendered
to the Porte by the Treaty of Belgrade, which reduced our annual
income by four or five million, and despite the long, costly, and
unfortunate war that added at least 20 million to the debt and
increased yearly interest alone by one million, the implementation
of the new financial system has fully covered the interest on that
debt and will even pay off part of the remaining balance each year.

Embassy expenses, salaries, pensions, and court costs were paid on
time, monthly or quarterly, even though the court costs increased a
bit owing to the numerous children conferred upon me by the grace
of God. The whole outstanding civil debt was divided, the greater
part being added to the military expenses and the remainder to the
fund attached to the military debt commission, which should be
completely paid off in a few years.

The 110,000 regulars, whom I maintain in readiness in the crownlands instead of the previous 60,000, receive their promised wages
from month to month, and those stationed in the German lands receive an additional share in hard currency. These advantages make
no service more attractive than ours. Since the last regulations, the
cavalry located in Hungary still is a little depressed, especially the
officers, but it receives its payment punctually, and I am willing to
provide a few extra financial benefits—at least to the lieutenants
and sergeants if not to all—as rewards to the men who have already
enlisted. The noncommissioned officers stationed in fortresses will
be paid every three months.

The field artillery has increased by a battalion and, because of
the diligent effort of Prince [Joseph Wenzel] Liechtenstein, has un-

doubtedly become much superior to what it used to be. This, of course, cost a bit more.

Improvements have also augmented the corps of engineers, both in numbers and in performance, and it is much better than it was earlier.

A larger annual sum will go to fortress construction, especially Petrovaradin, Timişoara, Olomouc, and the Spielberg. Likewise, more will go to the production of new firearms and artillery pieces to be distributed throughout the army.

Instead of a few *Grenzers* used for the most part only against the Turks, I have reorganized 47,000 into orderly regiments like the regulars, of whom one-third—over 15,000—can be assigned to any post of the army. This will cost more than 400,000 gulden annually.

I have provided sufficient funds to care for approximately 3,000 disabled veterans, who are assigned to the so-called veterans hospital in Pest. All others will be cared for in the villages in which they were born. Since the institution of the new system I have paid the expenses of all these men, who constitute approximately 17,000 in number, and in case of emergency, I have the advantage of ordering 7,000 and perhaps more of these men to garrison duty, thereby relieving the same number of regulars for field duty.

In all of the above, I have not mentioned one very important need, which concerns partly the education of the noble and non-noble youth through my establishment of the Theresian Academy, the local military academy; the Neustadt Cadet School; and the Pettau military orphanage. It also involves the elevation and cultivation of scholarship and knowledge, which serves both the reputation and honor of the court and the welfare and outlook of the people.

COMMERCE AND MANUFACTURE

During the early reform period, Maria Theresa recognized the importance of trade and industry to the improvement of the overall financial structure of her realm. An advocate of the eighteenth-century economic philosophy of mercantilism, she sponsored government promotion of commercial, manufacturing, and banking enterprises through loans, subsidies, and tax privileges, and employed high tariffs to protect them from foreign competition. To inspire business, in 1746 she created the General Directory of Economic Affairs (after 1749 the Directory of Commerce) and assigned to it and its commissions

*in the provinces the task of encouraging economic growth
throughout the Austrian and Bohemian lands. The following
document, addressed to the commercial commission for the
province of Lower Austria and dated January 4, 1754, describes
in general terms the methods the commissioners should use to
improve the economy of their land.*[5]

I am of the opinion that commercial affairs should be conducted more expeditiously and according to certain general principles. I suggest that the commission consider the following:

(1) In order to increase the spread of local industries and manufacture, the commission should become familiar with the present
condition of production, examine its weaknesses, consider possible
improvements, and act immediately on anything that appears to be
of great importance.

(2) Devote your constant attention to putting on a firm foundation new industries that improve our trade, so respectable retailers
and companies will thrive. Special attention should be given to
those manufacturers who serve either the processing of local products or the improving of our commerce abroad.

(3) For these beneficial undertakings, the commercial directory
will help all it can and will provide not only important protection,
but many substantial benefits to the retailers.

(4) You should oversee the flowering of Lower Austrian commerce
and pay particular notice to the export of domestic products abroad.
Preparations for greatly increased trade with Hungary and Turkey
and the passage of goods through Trieste should be made with
initiative and confidence. You should possess comprehensive knowledge of the condition of the land and its inhabitants in order to
make sure everyone knows that you will provide the necessary suggestions and the support of the motherly sentiments of the empress
for the welfare of the province. After these preparations, concern
yourselves with making easier the exploitation and export of each
land's natural products so that a flourishing trade among the crownlands will again be promoted. Nothing is more natural than that
the surplus of one crownland be traded to another.

But commerce cannot exist, much less improve, without good
transportation, so great attention must be paid to bettering the

[5] Adolf Beer, "Die österreichische Handelspolitik unter Maria Theresia und
Josef II," *Archiv für österreichische Geschichte*, LXXXVI (1899), 124–26. Translated by the editor.

roads, keeping those who build them earnestly at work, and making available the necessary construction material. You must keep a most careful eye on the plans and growth of the manufacturers, who receive considerable advantages through commercial and tax benefits. With the most diligent ardor the deputation there must examine the heart of a useful commerce and above all improve the present condition of the local factories and artisans, expose obvious defects, secure a thorough knowledge of the useful raw materials in the land itself or obtainable from the other crownlands, discover the genius of the people, how their way of life is organized, and what we can expect from their industry and talent. All proposals must be made with careful thought, so that the empress may depend upon them with confidence. Encourage not only the newly established factories in your province but also the other manufacturing works flourishing there.

(5) Be especially attentive toward increasing the export of local goods that have considerable demand abroad, so when international markets are available, good quality, price-worthy wares can bring a respectable price that will please the merchants and manufacturers specializing in foreign trade. The commission should particularly observe manufacturers in wool, silk, flax, woolen cloth, and all minerals and metals.

LAW

In the second reform period, which began toward the end of the Seven Years' War, Maria Theresa and her advisers focused more attention on the welfare of her subjects than on the basic military, financial, and administrative changes needed to strengthen the state. Among the reforms of this period was the codification of the civil and criminal law; made necessary by the extremely diverse legal traditions existing among the crownlands, it was authorized by the empress in 1752. Despite years of collection, synthesis, and debate, however, neither a uniform civil nor criminal code emerged during Maria Theresa's reign, largely owing to disagreements among various court factions as to what each code should include. The following passage contains the introduction and two articles of the Nemesis Theresiana, *the criminal code finished in 1768 but never introduced because of severe opposition from the co-regent Joseph, Chief Minister Kaunitz, and other important officials. These opponents especially criticized the code's con-*

tinued sanction of torture and the aggravated death penalty,
two punishments the empress strongly favored. Not until 1776
did Maria Theresa consent to the abolition of torture, but the
code was still unpublished upon her death in 1780.[6]

We, Maria Theresa, . . . send our greeting to each and all
higher and lower courts, city and provincial courts, capital courts,
masters of county courts, and administrations that exist in our royal
Bohemian, as well as our Lower, Inner, Upper, and Fore [Vorlände]
Austrian crownlands, and especially to all our truly loyal subjects
and inhabitants, whatever their property, station, birth, or occupation, and direct each and all to know the following: that we, among
other of our organs of government, have directed our careful attention—not only during times of serene peace but also during the
most awful war—to making certain that in our crownlands the
honor of God is secure as much through the introduction and maintenance of good morals and virtuous behavior as through the pre-
vention and extermination of all vices injurious to the land and
offensive to God. Hereafter we wish to administer as carefully as
possible the beneficial justice that promotes the general welfare by
means of protecting property and averting as well as punishing
crimes.

During our reign we have observed that, for the most part, continuous obstacles stand in the way of the orderly course of justice
in criminal matters.

(1) In each one of our crownlands there exists, for the most part,
a different criminal code for proceedings as well as for the punishment of criminals. In addition, there are variations in capital court
orders, some following the code of Emperor Charles, some that of
Ferdinand, some that of Leopold, some that of Joseph, in a few
places that of old provincial law, and finally in cases where provincial law is obscure or defective, that of Roman law. Such disunity
of provincial law has fallen so hard upon us and our administration
that we and our bureaucracy have found it necessary to have before
us one or another code—depending on the crownland—at each
criminal case brought before our court. In contrast nothing can be
more natural, reasonable, orderly, or beneficial to justice than the
creation of a single law for all the fraternal crownlands ruled by a

---

[6] *Constitutio Criminalis Theresiana* (Vienna: Johann Thomas Edlen von Tratt-
nern, 1769), Introduction, 174–75, 243–44. Translated by the editor.

single monarch. With such a law, our advisers, legal specialists, and all provincial administrators will be in the position that when they, by request, are assigned to a necessary service in this or any other crownland (or wanting better advantages and conveniences, they move their home from one to another of our provinces), they will become fit for service in all places and not be required to spend much time learning another or other special provincial law codes.

(2) In the previously mentioned capital court regulations, you will find noticeable variations, partly in major matters that are absolutely requisite for the completeness of procedures dealing with criminal jurisdiction, partly in the detailed discourses on legal policy particularly concerning the aggravating or mitigating circumstances of crimes, but primarily in the required instructions determining what regulations and procedure should be used, from beginning to end, in the prosecution of each kind of criminal case. And certainly (3) For the substitution or improvement of these variations as well as those of our most praiseworthy ancestors, we ourselves have from time to time issued numerous innovations in criminal law. But even these supplemental laws were issued in no orderly collection, and therefore remain for the most part unknown to newly assigned judges. Furthermore, these appended laws have been introduced in each crownland in order to conform with the provincial capital court regulations; consequently, these newer laws have reflected the inequities of the provincial criminal ordinances. As a result, the exact supervision of so many different regulations has become very difficult for us and our administrators, and improvements in criminal procedure have been greatly hindered.

In order to eliminate these and similar detrimental and restraining obstacles and frailties in our worthy judicial system, criminal procedure in all our German crownlands—its instigation and preparations, its complete discharge of criminal processes, the judgment of the criminal, and the execution of the sentence—will be handled as much as possible according to uniform legal principles and with equal dispatch.

So with the best intentions, we created a special court commission under the presidency of Michael Joseph Althann, our worthy privy councilor, knight of the Golden Fleece, and vice-president of our supreme justice ministry, with the most worthy instructions to inspect the various existing criminal ordinances along with the supplementary laws, to select the most natural and most reasonable of these, to correct variations and discrepancies, and thereby to create a new uniform criminal code with the general welfare of our crown-lands in mind. This commission had to present its findings to us for our final review and for our maternal decision; it has finally done so.

And now we have examined this improved criminal court regulation favorably and thoroughly, and find it composed properly. After extensive discussion, we wish that these ordinances be established with correct understanding and, by authority of our princely sovereignty, in the degree, manner, and form as hereby follows from article to article, and that these be the correct guiding principles in all criminal cases in all of our German crownlands. Likewise, all previous decisions, regulations, usages, traditions, and customs that run contrary to our general criminal code shall be abolished and put aside, and we hereby earnestly command that in criminal cases all provincial laws must conform to our general criminal code only —or to whatever clarifications we might make in this code on the basis of specific cases in the future. Our criminal code will become binding one year after its official publication. We command most earnestly that all citizens and inhabitants of our German crown-lands observe in all cases this criminal code; to fail to do so will invite serious repercussions. This is especially true for the authorities of the high and low courts who are most responsible for the exact observance and implementation of this general criminal code. No one shall handle criminal cases in any other way. This code will also be for everyone and for all crimes. Given in our imperial and royal capital of Vienna, the last day of December, 1768, twenty-ninth year of our reign.

ARTICLE 59: CONCERNING PERJURY AND FALSE WITNESS

Contents: (1) Definition of perjury. (2) Concerning special evidence and inquiries; perjury is a crime almost equivalent to a blasphemy of the Lord's name. (3) Punishment of a perjurer. (4) Aggravating circumstances. (5) Mitigating circumstances.

(1) False witness, or perjury, consists of a man willfully and fraudulently swearing to an untruth while claiming God as his witness. It constitutes a willfully given, false oath concerning some past or present event, or concerns someone's purposely telling untruths with some malicious end in view. Perjury also consists in someone's beginning with honest intentions and promising solemnly not to commit perjury, but in the end breaking his oath in a deliberate and dangerous way.

(2) Perjury is a form of blasphemy. The special evidence and in-

quiry included in Article 56 concerning blasphemy can be used in so far as the conditions of the case of false witness are similar.

(3) Punishment for intentional perjury is: First, usually execution by decapitation; this death penalty can be intensified according to conditions by extracting the tongue, cutting off the hand that swore the oath, or both. Second, the intensification of the punishment has special application for anyone who compounds his perjury by falsely accusing someone else of a capital crime in a court of law. Such false witness shall be punished with the same capital punishment the perjurer tried to inflict upon the other man. Third, in a case in which mitigating circumstances exist, we wish to concede to the careful consideration of the judge to choose a worthy punishment instead of death for the perjurer. Should the perjurer own no property, he will be expelled from all of our crownlands. Fourth, the punishment employed for perjury should also serve as the punishment for falsely taking an oath or breaking one's word when it leads to dangerous consequences. Point five understandably follows: Anyone who through his false witness or any other crime wounds or harms, in any way, his fellow man must make every effort to restore to the injured party his lost possessions and property, and is responsible for making good all outrages, damages, and expenses, and will be held to this by judicial recognizance.

(4) Aggravating circumstances that make perjury worse consist in the following: First, the guilty party has perjured himself often. Second, the guilty party is warned against perjury and is informed of its severe punishment but lies anyway. Third, perjury is done with excessive wickedness or daring. Fourth, an innocent party suffers torture, bodily harm, or irreparable damage. And most important, fifth, many people lose their possessions and property, or their honor, limb, or life.

(5) Mitigating circumstances, for which the punishment should be reduced, are: First, the person who swore the oath is a simpleton and did not sufficiently comprehend the seriousness of perjury. Second, someone swore to something out of ignorance. Third, he did not know or could not remember the punishment for perjury. Fourth, only little or no harm was done. Fifth, the perjurer can and will make good the damage he has done. Sixth, the person had honorable intentions and true purposes at the beginning when he took the oath, but later he violated his word by some indiscretion. Seventh and last, false accusations of perjury without a formal oath should be thrown out of court.

ARTICLE 89: Concerning the abandonment of children

Contents: (1) Two distinctions must be made concerning the abandonment of children. (2) What punishment should be used in each case. (3) Information that can be used as evidence. (4) Questions as to inquiries into cases. (5) Aggravating circumstances. (6) Mitigating circumstances.

(1) What punishment should be inflicted on those who do not seize their children with violent hands but in a determined and dangerous way put them in danger in order to get rid of them? One must observe the following two major distinctions in this matter.

The First: If a child is abandoned in a place far from communities and people so that he should suffer helplessly from hunger and exposure and die. The Second: If the child is abandoned not to put him in obvious danger of losing his life nor in some remote place, but at a spot which is well traveled so that either a person passing by or anyone else willing to be father to the child will embrace him, adopt him, and raise him. And if the mother did so to escape the punishment, disgrace, and ridicule of adultery or harlotry.

(2) In the first case the guilty will be executed by decapitation. If, however, the child is found still living and people will care for it, then the guilty party shall be treated with discretion, but still severely. In the other case, if the abandoned child (if abandoned against the will of the guilty) should die of hunger, frost, or some other cause, then the guilty party should suffer the full consequences or another severe punishment issued by the provincial courts. If this child is found living, the provincial court can decide how the guilty party will make amends. It is nevertheless necessary to observe that if, shortly after he is found, the child dies of causes connected with his abandonment, then the court must proceed with the punishment specified in the first part of this section under number (2).

(3) Evidence concerning such abandonment may consist in: First, if a mother in some malicious way tries to hide her pregnant condition or to procure an abortion, the court shall proceed as instructed in Article 2 above. Second, if an infant is found in a forest, open field, garden, public street or highway, or on water, and in the neighboring area a suspicious woman is found with engorged breasts. Third, if a suspicious person is seen in the area where the child was abandoned. Fourth, if the apparel in which the child is wrapped is found to belong to a suspected person or a name tag lying near the child is written in a suspect's handwriting.

(4) Inquiry can be made by following the same procedure as explained in previous articles.

(5) An aggravating circumstance, in which the crime appears even worse, is, among other things, primarily a case in which the guilty party has more than sufficient means to maintain the child, and none of the mitigating circumstances, which follow below, can be applied. In this case, we sincerely forbid any amnesty as set down in the preceding Article 87, No. 9, Verse 3. In case no orphanage or other means are available to nourish and raise the foundling, the local authorities will be responsible for overseeing the necessary means of bringing up the child.

(6) A mitigating circumstance that demands a milder punishment for the guilty party consists in a person's abandoning a child because of serious lack of food, abject poverty, naiveté, or unusual fear.

SCHOOLS

One area in which Maria Theresa took special interest was school reform, particularly at the elementary level. To outline plans for universal and compulsory education in the German part of her empire, she acquired the services of a recognized expert, John Joseph Felbinger, ironically a minister of Frederick the Great. Felbinger recommended the creation of elementary schools in each town and large village, high schools in cities and monasteries, and a teacher-training school in each province. Below are selected portions of the General School Regulation of December 6, 1774, based on Felbinger's recommendations. Despite numerous problems implementing these reforms, by Maria Theresa's death in 1780 approximately 500 new schools had opened.[7]

We, Maria Theresa, . . . offer to each and all of our loyal citizens and subjects of our realm and provinces, whatever their position of wealth may be, our grace and present the following for their observation.

Because nothing is so dear to us as the welfare of those lands entrusted to our administration by God, and since we are accustomed

---

[7] Anton Weiss, *Das Werden unserer Volkschule* (Leipzig, Prague, Vienna: Schulwissenschaftliche Verlag A. Haase, 1918), pp. 61–66, 72–73, 74–76. Translated by the editor.

to paying strict attention to their best possible improvement, so we hold it true that the education of youth of both sexes, which is the most important foundation for the true happiness of the nation, deserves a thorough examination.

This matter has drawn our attention all the more because the future life of all people, the molding of the spirit and mentality of the whole community, certainly depend on good education and guidance in the early years. This can never be achieved unless the darkness of ignorance is enlightened by thorough teaching and learning devices and each person is assured an education suitable to his station. To achieve this necessary and useful end, we have established general school regulations for all our German crownlands and provinces.

1. In order to bring the whole school system into suitable order and to insure that it always remain in such order, we hereby decree that in every province of our kingdoms a single school commission should be created by the local administration. This commission should consist of two, but preferably three, if practical, local administrators, an official from the *Ordinariat,* and a secretary—with the director of the normal school serving as assistant. These members must be approved by us. Although we are determined from time to time to give to this commission memoranda concerning its activity, it generally will have the task of assuming responsibility for the construction and administration of the German schools of its province, including the appointment and regulation of teachers, as well as day-to-day school affairs. In the future it must see to the retention of the prescribed way of teaching, as well as the operation and execution of our general orders, and from time to time it will send to us its informative and authoritative reports concerning the advancement of the school system and the events affecting our decisions.

2. The general German schools should be of three kinds: normal schools, high schools, and community, or elementary, schools.

Normal schools are those schools which provide the guidelines for all other schools in the province. Therefore, in each province only one normal school should exist, and it should reside in the same location as the school commission so that it can direct all other schools of the province. These schools should train the teachers for the other German schools, instruct them in all necessary subjects, or at least rigorously test those trained elsewhere if they should wish to teach in the province. In order to teach all the prescribed subject matter, every normal school must include a director and four or five teachers, among whom must be a religious instructor.

German high schools will be established in large cities and, where the opportunity exists, in monasteries. To insure proper distribution, at least one such high school must be available in every quarter, circle, or district of the province.

General, or elementary, schools should be located in small cities and market villages, and in the country, at least in all places where there exists a parish church or a mission church affiliated with but distant from a parish church.

3. The purpose here is by no means to create all these schools from scratch or to produce all new teachers. Instead, the already existing schools should be reorganized and the already employed school personnel instructed according to the regulations determined for our crownlands. Should the school commission see fit to appoint new school personnel, however, no one who has been connected with instruction in the school earlier may obtain a school office or position unless he is fully knowledgeable of the prescribed educational regulations and has been approved by the normal school on the basis of his performance in the examinations given him. Also the right to establish schools and to instruct the youth remains the same as before for all schools, whether they be secular or religious, for males or females. These schools, however, must conform in their structure as much as possible and without exception to the rules established by the school commission of the province in which they are founded. Furthermore, each of these schools must follow the commission's rulings concerning the method of teaching, subject matter, and special instruction.

From now on, completely new schools shall be established only at those places where none exists but where one is required, or in places where the youth are so numerous that they would have to be excluded from existing schools. In such cases the community will bear most of the cost, since it will derive the most benefit. Because it will gain respectable and useful citizens, however, the government will also take part in financing new schools depending on need. Allocations will be judged according to the necessity of the construction itself and the required increase in teachers. . . .

8. Each teacher must instruct all students together in one classroom. To use class reading time effectively, he should make use of

tables and other reading methods as prescribed. In short, he must follow exactly that which is contained in the books of methods passed out for the instruction of teachers. Instruction must not concentrate immediately on committing things to memory or on plaguing the children with rote learning of necessities but on improving their understanding. Make everything understandable to them, and they will learn to extract knowledge slowly and thoroughly.

9. Students of different ages and sex who are learning the same subjects are to be brought together in one class and then divided according to the ability of the students so that the best, the middle, and the worst can progress together. Each of these groups can then be treated according to its needs by the teacher, who will find the appropriate instructions for each in the books of methods he will receive. In every school there will exist as many classes as there are teaching subjects, and every class can be divided even further according to the ability of the students. . . .

11. Although the elements of a subject taught in a school course will be presented so that the students thoroughly comprehend them, a few pupils may still exist—as is especially likely in writing classes—who will not have learned enough and, in practice, have not achieved the required results. Such students must repeat the course or take additional courses. . . .

12. Children of both sexes who live in cities and whose parents or guardians lack either the will or the means to retain their own tutors belong without exception in school as soon as they have passed six years of age. From then on they must attend the German schools until they achieve the necessary education for their future occupation and way of life. They should hardly be able to complete this program by their twelfth year if they begin in or after their sixth year. Therefore, we look favorably on parents' enrolling their children in the German schools for at least six or seven years. They can attend longer according to their will or need. But if a few wish to move on to advanced studies or to leave school before their twelfth year, they must pass the regular examinations and obtain a written statement from the principal that they have adequately learned everything required. Where circumstances permit the establishment of a few schools for young girls, the girls should attend them and, if it is deemed suitable, should also learn sewing, knitting, and other crafts appropriate to their sex. . . .

SERFDOM

In the latter years of her reign, the empress became increasingly concerned with the problem of serf reform. Throughout much of the empire, the peasants remained essentially chattels of their lords, obligated to pay monetary and work dues that frequently kept them in a state of total subjection. Motivated by reasons of economics (a successful peasant pays higher taxes), fear of social revolution, and undoubtedly humanitarianism, during the late 1760s and 1770s Maria Theresa authorized a number of commissions to investigate the conditions of the serfs in various crownlands and to recommend reforms. The result included a series of so-called Robot Patents (serf labor dues were known as robot *taken from the general Slavic word for work), designed to regulate the peasants' labor payments in virtually all of the Habsburg lands. The following selections, which clearly express Maria Theresa's wish to alleviate the serfs' plight in Bohemia, come not from these patents but from letters written in 1777 to her son Ferdinand.*[8]

This will be short. Not the carnival [pre-Lenten celebration] but affairs in Bohemia concern me now, especially the plans to create a permanent system there. Not that any disturbance or disobedience has erupted yet, but we can expect it in the summer unless we institute certain reforms. The peasants there are crushed under the excesses of the lords, who, in my thirty-six years of rule, have always known how to sabotage changes and how to hold their serfs in bondage. If only the emperor would stay neutral—not even support me—in this affair, I could abolish personal serfdom and forced labor, and everything would quiet down. But unfortunately these men, seeing I will no longer put up with them, have joined the emperor, and the resulting disputes, which now are widespread, have disturbed me greatly. Provided that benefits result, I want to say nothing about all that he costs me, but I am often depressed about it. . . .

You are now in the full celebration of your carnival, and we have begun paying penance. The beginning always is the hardest. Fur-

[8] Maria Theresa to Ferdinand, January 30 and February 13, 1777, in Alfred von Arneth, ed., *Briefe der Kaiserin Maria Theresia an ihre Kinder und Freunde* (Vienna: Wilhelm Braumüller, 1881), II, 66–67, 69–70. Translated by the editor.

thermore, the general situation in Europe worries me. I am deeply disturbed about our affairs in Bohemia, even more so because the emperor and I cannot agree on reforms. The oppression and tyranny inflicted upon those poor people are known and verified; we must establish a more equitable system there. I was ready to authorize the necessary reforms, when all at once the lords—who, by the way, are all ministers—caused the emperor to hesitate and in one blow annulled all the work of the last two years. I hope that the measures now in force will suffice to restore calm and obedience, but I fear a revolution. These people, without hope for the future, have nothing to lose and thus are to be feared. But, while demanding obedience, I hope at the same time to give them relief. Others have argued that I should wait until they deserve it, but necessity is not the law. . . .

3
Foreign Affairs

Throughout Maria Theresa's reign foreign affairs competed closely with internal reform for the center of her attention. Upon her succession to the throne, foreign policy rested in the hands of Count Sinzendorf, a man of such stature —albeit questionable ability and integrity—that Maria Theresa felt reluctant to oppose him. Upon his death in 1742 the empress assumed personal guidance of policy, although she did establish an independent foreign ministry whose president, Count Uhlfeld, could and did offer advice. Maria Theresa's personal direction continued until 1753, when she appointed as head of foreign affairs Count Kaunitz, her brilliant, loyal adviser, confidant, and friend until the end of her days. From 1753 to 1765 Kaunitz and the empress jointly guided the diplomacy of the Habsburg state. After 1765 Joseph II also participated, although not always agreeably.

REVERSAL OF ALLIANCES

Undoubtedly the most famous success of Maria Theresa and Kaunitz was the diplomatic revolution of 1756 in which Austria abandoned its traditional friend Britain for a military alliance with its traditional enemy France. Although Austria and France had been discussing such a union for some years, it did not become a reality until May, 1756, four months after Britain, the old friend of Austria, and Prussia, had concluded a friendship treaty of their own. Under the circumstances, Kaunitz believed it only natural that France and Austria should join together in opposition. The conclusion of the Austro-French treaty set the stage for the Seven Years' War, which erupted in the summer of 1756 with Austria, France, and Russia arrayed against Prussia and Britain. The following passage includes an interview between the empress and the British ambassador to Vienna, Robert Keith, who endeavors to learn the nature of the new association between the two powers while expressing disbelief that Austria and France

have truly reconciled their differences. In reply, Maria Theresa
sets forth the reasons for the change of allies.[1]

In an audience of the empress, the British minister experienced greater affability and condescension; but she expressed the
utmost abhorrence of a connection with the king of Prussia; and
notwithstanding her previous negotiation with France, threw the
blame of first deserting the ancient alliance on the king of England.
In reply to the observation of Mr. Keith, that the answer delivered
by count Kaunitz contained an absolute renunciation of the ancient
and true system of Europe, she said, "I have not abandoned the old
system, but Great Britain has abandoned me and that system, by
concluding the Prussian treaty, the first intelligence of which struck
me like a fit of apoplexy. I and the king of Prussia are incompatible;
and no consideration on earth shall ever induce me to enter into
any engagement of which he is a party." Mr. Keith, after apologizing
for the treaty, and employing many arguments to reconcile the
empress-queen, adverted to the supposed negotiation with the
French court. She refused to explain her conduct; but asked, "Why
should you be surprised, if, following your example in concluding
a treaty with Prussia, I should enter into an engagement with
France?"
Affecting to disbelieve that the empress would connect herself
with the inveterate enemy of her person and family, the British
minister declared that nothing could convince him of the existence
of such an alliance, till he saw with his own eyes the signature of
MARIA THERESA at the bottom of a treaty with that crown. "I
am," she replied, "far from being French in my disposition, and do
not deny that the court of Versailles has been my bitterest enemy;
but I cannot conceal, that the cessions which Great Britain extorted
from me at the peace of Dresden, and of Aix-la-Chapelle, have
totally disabled me. I have little to fear from France; I am unable
to act with vigor and have no other recourse than to form such
arrangements as will secure what remains." The British minister ex-
claiming, "Will you, the empress and archduchess, so far humble
yourself as to throw yourself into the arms of France?" "Not into
the arms," she rejoined, "but on the side of France." "I have," she
continued, "hitherto signed nothing with France, though I know not

[1] William Coxe, *History of the House of Austria*, 3rd ed. (London: Henry G.
Bohn, 1854), III, 363–65.

what may happen; but whatever happens, I promise, on my word of honour, not to sign anything contrary to the interest of your royal master, for whom I have a most sincere friendship and regard."

The empress listened with great affability to all the remonstrances and arguments of the British minister, but continued unshaken in her resolution: and concluded: "I no longer have it in my power to take an active share in distant transactions; I am therefore little concerned for the remote parts of my dominions, and my principal object is to secure my hereditary possessions. I have truly but two enemies whom I really dread, the king of Prussia and the Turks; and while I and the empress of Russia continue on the same good terms as now subsist between us, we shall, I trust, be able to convince Europe, that we are in a condition to defend ourselves against those adversaries, however formidable."

The empress gave this audience on the 13th of May, and the treaty with France had been already signed on the 1st. In imitation of the convention of London, the two sovereigns agreed, by an act of neutrality, to prevent the contest in America from disturbing their mutual harmony; and a treaty of alliance, purely defensive, renewed all former engagements since the treaty of Westphalia. The empress-queen promised to defend the French dominions in Europe, if attacked, except during the present war with England; while the king of France was to aid the house of Austria without an exception. The two powers also stipulated to assist each other with a mutual succour of 24,000 men in case of invasion, the present war excepted.

FIRST PARTITION OF POLAND

One of the most serious diplomatic crises in Maria Theresa's later years was the first partition of Poland, a complicated affair involving a Polish internal upheaval, a Russo-Turkish war, and fears on the part of both Austria and Prussia that Russia was becoming too powerful. Vienna's policy, directed by Joseph II and Kaunitz, included among other things, a premature and ill-considered occupation of a Polish province in January, 1771, and in July of the same year, a secret convention with the Ottoman Empire to block Russian aggrandizement. To prevent a possible clash between Austria and Russia, Frederick the Great suggested that each of the three powers (Austria, Prussia, and Russia) annex a portion of Poland and that Russia receive minor gains at the expense of the Ottoman Empire. The resulting partition caused the empress much anxi-

ety because, although she knew Austria could not stand by and watch Prussia and Russia divide Poland between them, she could scarcely bear the thought of annexing land to which she had little or no claim, thus committing the very crime for which she had vilified Frederick for over thirty years. In the end she relented, however, and her dynasty won the Polish province of Galicia, which remained a Habsburg possession until the end of the First World War. In the following three selections, one a memorandum on the crisis[2] and the other two letters to her sons, Maria Theresa provides insights into her own dilemma and the difficulties of Austrian policy in this matter.

Everything depends upon our reasonable withdrawal from this complicated affair. Indeed, it would be even better to end it with no concrete advantages.

Every day is important, or else all will be concluded to our disappointment and injury; to our disadvantage the three powers—Russia, Prussia, and the Porte—will unite against us, which will result in our inevitable displacement in Poland. We shall be ejected from there in a totally dishonorable way unless we at least reach some sort of understanding with Prussia. God prevents us from encouraging war any longer and inciting the Turks, so that we must pledge to provide them with military help because of their unfortunate bankruptcy. Where there still remains truth and faith—upon that everything still depends.

But the greatest mistake is that this affair, at least the way I see it, has assumed a completely false supposition, namely that war or peace is up to us.

I immediately dispatched a courier to Constantinople to advise the Turks to conclude an armistice and even a peace; I went to work again with Zegelin [the Prussian ambassador], and at the same moment sent another courier through Berlin to St. Petersburg to pronounce clearly in both places that I wish peace and will devote everything here to achieve it. But if Russia or Prussia wants to secure a few advantages in Poland, I cannot view it with indifference but must have a clear statement about their policies. In this case I cannot withdraw empty-handed, although it is of little convenience for me to win anything at the expense of Poland or the Porte. The king

---

[2] Adolf Beer, *Die erste Teilung Polens* (Vienna: Carl Gerold's Sohn, 1873), III, 340–41. Translated by the editor.

of Prussia must also compensate us, either with Galicia, some Frank-
ish territory, or even some lands in Cleves, because I will take nothing from the Turks. I make no secret of our active alliance with the
Porte.

Through this clear and candid statement, I believe—and I find
myself alone in this—that we can come out of this affair with honor
and perhaps even some profit or at least limited disadvantages. I advised the Turks, in light of their great weakness, above all to seek
peace, and I would gladly free them from the payment of the stipulated millions they owe us if I could convince them to surrender
Belgrade. In present circumstances it is not a question of possessing
more or less, but how one can get out of the affair with the least
injury. This must occur, however, without losing time.

Maria Theresa to Joseph, January, 1772[3]

I am sufficiently concerned about our critical situation to examine
it one more time in all its ramifications and try to find a remedy, if
not good, at least not too bad. It is most important for us to secure
peace everywhere as quickly as possible. By prolonging the crisis, our
situation becomes increasingly unfortunate. It is no longer possible
to return to our earlier policy after our first false steps (and I consider false everything we have done since the month of November,
1770, when the withdrawal of troops from Italy and the Low Countries was resolved) and since the unfortunate convention we signed
with the Turks. Our excessively menacing tone toward the Russians and our mysterious conduct regarding our allies as well as our
adversaries indicate that we have decided to try to profit from the
war between the Porte and Russia in order to extend our frontiers
and to obtain advantages we never even considered before the conflict. We want to act like the Prussians and at the same time retain
the appearance of honesty. By trying to do so, we are deluding ourselves as to the means, and are confusing appearances and events.
It is possible that I deceive myself and that these events are favorable and that I am unable to perceive them. But should they win
for us the district of Wallachia, Belgrade even, I would regard them
always as purchased too dearly—at the expense of our honor, the
glory of the monarchy, and our good faith and religion.

During my unfortunate reign we have at least tried to pursue true

[3] Maria Theresa to Joseph II, January, 1772, in Alfred von Arneth, ed., *Maria
Theresia und Joseph II: Ihre Correspondenz* (Vienna: Carl Gerold's Sohn, 1867),
I, 362–63. Translated by the editor.

and equitable policies in all affairs and to maintain good faith, moderation, and fidelity in our engagements. This has earned for us the confidence, dare I say even the admiration, of Europe and the respect and veneration of our enemies. In one year all this is lost. I insist that I have tried to sustain it, and that nothing in the world has cost me more dearly than the loss of our good name. Unfortunately, I must emphasize especially to you that we deserved it, and I wish that we might remedy this situation by rejecting as evil and ruinous all efforts to profit from these troubles and that we deliberate how to get out of this difficult affair as quickly as possible with the least ill effects, without thinking of acquisitions for ourselves but only of the restoration of our credit and good faith and, as much as possible, the balance of power.

Maria Theresa to Archduke Ferdinand, September 12, 1772 [4]

[Count Charles Gotthard] Firmian [minister in Milan] received a long report concerning our present situation, our relations with Russia, Prussia, and the Turks, and above all concerning the unfortunate partition of Poland, which cost me ten years. You will see the whole, wretched unfolding of this matter. How long have I resisted it! Only the defeats of the Turks, following each other blow by blow; the hopelessness of winning aid from France or England; the possibility of having to fight alone against Russia and Prussia; and the misery, hunger, and ruinous sicknesses in my lands compelled me to follow these unholy proposals, which throw a shadow over my whole reign. God will that I not be held responsible for them in the next world. I confess to you that I find no end to this business; it lies in my heart, follows me, and poisons my already too tragic days. I must stop writing about this matter in order not to excite myself too much lest I fall into the blackest melancholy. . . .

I tenderly kiss you both [Ferdinand and his wife] and remain always your true mother.

THE POTATO WAR

The last great diplomatic achievement of Maria Theresa's long reign came in the War of the Bavarian Succession of 1778, more commonly known as the Potato War because, dur-

[4] Maria Theresa to Archduke Ferdinand, September 17, 1772, in Alfred von Arneth, ed., *Briefe der Kaiserin Maria Theresia an ihre Kinder und Freunde* (Vienna: Wilhelm Braumüller, 1881). I, 150. Translated by the editor.

ing the winter of 1778–79, to avoid starvation soldiers on both sides dug frozen potatoes out of the ground. The war began when Joseph II and Kaunitz tried to secure by peaceful means, a large portion of Bavaria upon the death of its ruler. When their negotiations ran into difficulty, Joseph ordered his troops to occupy part of that country. In response, Frederick the Great, who had little desire to see Austria strengthened by the annexation of Bavaria, enlisted the cooperation of some of the German princes to protest the occupation and advanced his own troops to the Bohemian frontier. Talks to settle the matter lasted throughout the spring of 1778, but when Joseph rejected the final Prussian proposal in June, Frederick ordered his armies across the border. At this moment, Maria Theresa, who had pleaded with her son to avoid a conflict, intervened decisively. Unbeknownst to Joseph, she dispatched to Frederick, by special messenger, a personal letter requesting the resumption of negotiations and including a list of concessions she knew would satisfy the Prussian monarch. This letter is presented below.[5]

My Brother and Cousin:

With the recall of Baron Riedesel [Prussian ambassador in Vienna] and the invasion of the troops of Your Majesty, I recognize with the most extreme feeling of regret the outbreak of a new war. My age and my inclination to maintain peace are known to all the world, and I can give you no truer indication of this feeling than by this act that I now commit. My maternal heart is rightly alarmed to see two of my sons and a beloved son-in-law with the army. I write this letter without having informed my son the emperor, and I plead with you to keep it secret, for its success may depend on it. My wishes are that the negotiations, conducted up to this hour through His Majesty the Emperor and which, to my greatest regret, have broken off, be resumed and proceed to a conclusion. Baron [Francis Maria] Thugut, who is furnished with instructions and authority, will personally lay this note in your hands. I earnestly wish that the enclosed articles can fulfill our wishes to our honor and our satisfaction, and I ask you to answer with the same feelings my sincere

[5] Maria Theresa to Frederick of Prussia, July 12, 1778 in Friedrich Walter, ed., *Maria Theresia: Briefe und Aktenstüke in Auswahl* (Darmstadt: Wissenschaftliche Buchgesellschaft, 1968), 451–52. Reprinted by permission of Wissenschaftliche Buchgesellschaft. Translated by the editor.

wishes for the lasting restoration of our good relations, to the betterment of mankind and our families. I am

Your Majesty's Good Sister and Cousin,

Maria Theresa

Postscript: The 12th

At this moment news from the 8th and 9th has come from the army, which announces to me your offensive against us. I hasten that much more to dispatch the above before some event changes the present circumstances. After the departure of Thugut, I intend to send a courier to the emperor and to instruct him, without going into details and thereby preventing perhaps precipitate steps, what I wish in my whole heart.

KAUNITZ

As mentioned before, Maria Theresa's foremost adviser after 1753 was the able Count Kaunitz. Despite his virtually unassailable position, he seemed the antithesis of the kind of man who would appeal to the empress. Whereas she was deeply religious, he enjoyed the secularist, anticlerical ideas of the Enlightenment; whereas she preferred personal discipline and humility, he exuded laxity, arrogance, and vanity; whereas she loved fresh air and the cold, he so shunned the outdoors that he was carried to his appointments in an enclosed sedan chair so no breeze could reach him. Despite his eccentricities, she appreciated Kaunitz's ability and, as time went on, relied upon him for advice in virtually all matters, domestic and foreign. Though they worked well together, these two great politicians could not resist at times practicing the diplomatic arts of cajolery, bluff, and threat upon each other; indeed their own correspondence contains a number of Kaunitz's offers to resign and the empress's flattering responses to bring him back. The following letter, written on June 7, 1766, reveals Maria Theresa's ability to play on Kaunitz's vanity and loyalty to make him reconsider a resignation he had submitted ostensibly because of poor health but in reality because Joseph II refused to accept his advice on some matter.[6]

[6] Maria Theresa to Kaunitz, June 7, 1766, in Alfred von Arneth, *Geschichte Maria Theresias* (Vienna: Wilhelm Braumüller, 1876), VII, 300–04. Translated by the editor.

You have made the last twenty-four hours quite bitter for me. Because my heart was affected too harshly, I did not want to follow my first inclinations, but allowed myself instead additional time so my reason could come to my aid. After thorough reflection, I, as monarch and friend, now send this resignation back to you and wish for all time not to know its contents. As monarch I cannot allow such a step, and at the same time I offer you all necessary assistance and every consideration in order to preserve your valuable life. You must realize that my trust in you was never more complete than now. You have seen that in the difficult circumstances in which I find myself, my first thought was to depend on you, and nothing concerns my heart more than that your trust will be held so completely by my son as it is by me.

I also must confess that to me it is entirely acceptable that my son, as the first reports are suggesting, did not favor you right away. And at this moment you want to leave me—you who so often has preached to me not to loose the reins of monarchy from my hands. Does it follow that you, ten months later, will abandon me without any adequate reason? Earlier I understood your devotion, but not any longer. Is it jealousy, is it distrust? Are evil tongues or false rumors responsible? Is it my own failings? If so, why do you not say so? My faults are certainly not so great that on their account I deserve your leaving without even listening to me. They can spring only from my declining years, from my low spirits, but can never be rooted in a change of my character. You know how often I have asked you to tell me of my weaknesses. Indeed I regret that you have done it so infrequently. It must have been necessary because I can only blame my own failings for your now wanting to leave as soon as possible, without warning me in the slightest way or explaining yourself more thoroughly. At this moment and in light of all the assistance that I offer to you now and have offered to you always, the only reason that you give—that of your health—could not have caused such a rash decision. I have nothing more to add. Could Kaunitz's heart have been gripped by base jealousy? Could it have doubted my own heart, feared some change of mind, or believed superficial gossip? Imagine how much my soul and mind have felt sickened that in this matter you consider me suspicious of the slightest blunder on your part. But that is my fate. Never do I find explanations from my friends; always I find myself abandoned by them. In my miserable life I have experienced enough discomfort, which is illustrated best by the alienation of those upon whom I depended completely. Please explain how this misfortune happens to me. Before you become disgusted with me, you should tell me why this occurs. Even more so you have the right to do it, because I entrusted to you the secrets of my heart, my weaknesses, and my faults; I lived contentedly knowing I could depend on you.

How very unfortunate are we that we can have no true friend. I thought I had one; I was quiet and peaceful; consider my disappointment. I imagine you would think you could fool another, but not me, who has had time enough to become acquainted with human nature. I am indulgent and good-natured; yes, I can even say I am unable to be forever angry, and I can forget matters completely. I find myself in this mood now. As earlier, I offer to you my complete friendship and full trust. Never shall you hear reproaches from me; I have now said everything, and my anger is gone. I cannot say the same for my disappointment, but I shall get over it. The only condition that I request is that you present an oral and written explanation concerning any misgivings you still harbor about my policy or my person, and that you never listen to others concerning either. You deserve this peace of mind in order to serve the state usefully, to support me, and to educate the people who, after our deaths, will be able to perform services to the state as valuable as we have striven to perform. Either we die with our weapons in our hands, or we shall hide ourselves in the gloomy mountains of the Tyrol, there to end our sad lives, abandoned and forgotten by everyone. This alone your sovereign chooses to advise and command you.

4
Family

Of all her accomplishments, none provided Maria Theresa more pleasure than her large family. From her marriage to Francis Stephen of Lorraine in 1736 to the birth of her last child in 1756, she bore sixteen children of whom ten reached adulthood. As her offspring grew up, she engaged in a voluminous correspondence with them, in which she uttered her opinions on virtually every matter, from popular intellectual currents to the number of times each child should go to confession and Mass. Throughout, she revealed a sensitivity, wisdom, and discipline that can scarcely be matched.

HER HUSBAND

Maria Theresa's first and foremost love throughout her life was her husband, Francis Stephen of Lorraine. The empress herself dated her infatuation with him from the age of six—when he was fifteen—and she remained completely devoted to him during his life; after his death she mourned his passing until her own final days. Despite this love for him, and the fact that after 1745 he was Holy Roman emperor, she never allowed him a decisive voice in affairs of state; she kept the power for herself. Nonetheless, Francis Stephen was by no means an incompetent; he won a reputation as a superb businessman and, when allowed to rule personally as he did in his own duchy of Tuscany, showed himself able and well-liked by his subjects. In the following passages, both written shortly after his death—one a letter to a personal friend, the other a page from her prayer book—Maria Theresa reveals the extent of her love for her husband and her deep sorrow at his loss.[1]

---

[1] Maria Theresa to Countess Sophia Amalia Enzenberg, February 12, 1766 in Arneth, ed., *Briefe der Kaiserin Maria Theresia an ihre Kinder und Freunde* (Vienna: Wilhelm Braumüller, 1881), IV, 468–70. Translated by the editor.

My dear Enzenberg:

Only a year ago this was the happiest day of my life [her wedding anniversary]; it still is because this happiness is imprinted in my saddened heart and will not cease until I die. But actually the sweet is now mixed with the bitter. I have found great consolation today in the ashes [February 12 was Ash Wednesday]; my lot I accept with great eagerness. I have passed this happy day alone with my thoughts, locked in my study, surrounded by portraits of our dear illustrious master; here again can I nourish myself with true affection. All these hours I have thought about my past happiness, not without bitter regret that I failed to take full advantage of it during the time I had it. The thirty years, which end today, appear to me only ten, while the five months since his death seem twenty years.

Today you have seen the Mass vestments made from his worthy sleeping gown. I also have one here, which renews for me his memory, and, to celebrate this day, I have ordered mine placed in my closet. All that I have left is my grave. I await it with impatience because only it will reunite me with the sole object that my heart has loved in this world and which has been the object and goal of all my deeds and sentiments. You realize the void in my life since he has left. I am all the more discouraged because I believed I could find solace only by throwing myself more than ever into my work and and thus blunting my misery by not giving myself time to think about or feel my condition.

The good Lord has taken from me two other persons who possessed good judgment and my confidence, Haugwitz and Daun. Both were good Christians, zealous, and devoted; both true friends who have told me the truth promptly and to whom I could open my heart with ease. I now lack this consolation also. It appears to me that the good Lord has taken pity on my soul, which needs repose in order to do penance and find salvation. I think more than ever of retiring to my dear Innsbruck. I believe that I will find my peace of mind only there where I left it [Francis Stephen died in Innsbruck]. This letter repeats itself from day to day, but I know your devotion to me and I have no fear of causing you too much inconvenience. You must pardon my broken heart for this outpouring of grief.

I received the sermon with great pleasure and read through it twice; the anecdote you added made it even more touching. [The sermon Maria Theresa discussed was that delivered by a Franciscan eight days before the emperor's death, in which he tried to demonstrate the uncertainty of death.] We must marvel at the Divine Will, bow our heads, and hope that the good Lord, merciful as He is, will take pity on the worthy soul of our dear master. . . .

Entry from Maria Theresa's prayer book[2]

Emperor Francis, my husband, lived 56 years, 8 months, 10 days, and died on August 18, 1765, at 9:30 P.M. So he lived

Months	680
Weeks	2,958½
Days	20,778
Hours	496,992

My happy marriage lasted 29 years, 6 months, and 6 days. Since I gave him my hand around the same hour—and also on a Sunday—that he was so suddenly torn from me, our union continued 29 years, 334 months, 1,540 weeks, 10,781 days, 258,744 hours.

My years of rule: 28 years, 2 months, 12 days; so 338 months, 1,471 weeks, 10,300 days, 247,200 hours.

Should I pray so many paternosters, aves, requiems, and gloria patris or should I give so many alms?

HER SONS

Maria Theresa constantly offered advice to her children, not only as they grew up but long after they had reached adulthood, married, and produced families of their own. The following selection comes from a letter written in April, 1774, to her youngest son, Maximilian, who, at the age of seventeen and a half, was about to embark on a two-year "grand tour." In it she provides comments and offers guidance concerning a number of subjects for his immediate and future consideration, but most interesting are her views on the philosophy of the Enlightenment, the dominating intellectual movement of her century. In the middle of the letter she severely castigates the secular nature of the Enlightenment and decries its emphasis

[2] Alfred von Arneth, *Geschichte Maria Theresias* (Vienna: Wilhelm Braumüller, 1876), VII, 520. Translated by the editor.

on freedom, which she believes undermines the morality of the
youth.[3]

I confess that because of my love for you, it is a great sacrifice
to allow you to go abroad when you are still so young. I have decided, however, to do it anyway. Thinking only of your own welfare,
without considering my own feelings, I will sacrifice myself and allow you to go. Here you have nothing more to learn and have not
found the personal experiences to educate yourself or to realize the
value of that which I allowed taught to you. You will admit that I
have neglected nothing concerning your formal education and the
development of the gifts that God has bestowed upon you. In spite
of my age, my feebleness, and the concerns of state, the upbringing
of my children has always occupied my attention first and foremost.
If everything has not been carried out according to my orders and
instructions or with the carefulness that I apply to state affairs, it is
still not my fault, but only the result of those thousands of circumstances that allow us in this life to reach no true fulfillment and
which are inextricably bound to the corruptible and unlucky nature
of humanity. This is the case especially of the rulers of the earth
where so much depends on cooperation and where so often envy and
selfishness ruin the best measures.

Your great misfortune is that you lost your father so early in life.
At that time you were not yet nine years old, and you can no longer
remember the way he talked or acted, but only his appearance, and
even that you recall largely from the pictures that hang in all of my
and my children's rooms so that he will live always in our acts and
our hearts.

Since his death, everything here has changed; one could say that
neither a court nor a head of state really exists. I was so sunk in
grief that for the next two years I could not set myself to work, and
old age, grief, and the pressure of business exhausted my mental
and physical powers after my serious illness [smallpox]. The last unfortunate marriage of your brother the emperor and many other
circumstances contributed to this complete change. The mood that
prevails presently in Vienna is just as bad in matters of religion and
propriety as it is for the well-being of a family and especially for
the upbringing of young people, who here give themselves up to great

[3] Maria Theresa to Maximilian, undated [c. April, 1774] in Arneth, ed., *Briefe*
an ihre Kinder und Freunde, II, 317–39.

debauchery. From all this I intend to remove you, for you are at an age when, first stepping out of the bounds of childhood, one is scarcely able to control himself and the passions are the most dangerous. Your spiritual welfare and your future happiness depend on it. This view alone has inspired me to overcome my love for you and to give up the last pledge of my happy marriage, a happiness which, in the daily course of affairs, I will perhaps never again experience on this earth.

After the death of your father, whose loss hurt me so much more because I had been so happy, I preferred to live in the gloomy past. Nine years have I done so, and yet my grief has not stayed behind. Just the opposite, every moment opens my wounds afresh. They will never close, and only my children can provide a little consolation for me by trying to follow in his footsteps.

You are the youngest of them and the eighth archduke; to your good fortune—and that is great—you are not destined to rule. Therefore, your days can only be much more pleasant and you will have to compose that many fewer justifications for your actions. Nonetheless, owing to your status, you are obliged to give careful attention to everything that affects your person. In an honorable and appropriate manner, we have provided the following for your future: office of grand master of the German order; the *statthalter-ship* of Hungary, which your brother-in-law now possesses; and finally the property that your incomparable father left you, which includes Holitsch, Sassin, Gölding, Eckartsau, and Hof as well as their equivalent in gold. All this is yours when the emperor and I deem it appropriate.

The post in Hungary is one of the most important and at the same time the most agreeable in the whole empire: before the gates of Vienna and at the head of a people who, in my eyes, have acquired much merit, to whom I thank my existence on the throne of my ancestors, and who have, during the thirty-three years of my reign, manifested the greatest loyalty and the most eager willingness to support me and to carry out my wishes. If you do the same as I and show to them love and trust, then you will be convinced that there is much resourcefulness in this people. For this understanding, as for so many things, I thank your late father, who alone judged the Hungarians correctly. And if one handles them in the future as I have done, I hope that you yourself will be happy by making them happy. By doing so you will show that you are our worthy son. Still, understand this only in so far as it concerns the office of *statthalter,* which is completely subordinate to the orders of the sovereign. As to the other gifts, the grand master of the German order is a pleasant appointment and a quite adequate position, and it is always good to have a little something to call one's property.

Then what has an eighth archduke to expect generally? *The higher your birth, the more critical your situation.* Regard this eighth-highest position as your greatest fortune and do not abdicate it frivolously, generally never, unless your house approves or demands it, because you will be dependent upon and obedient to him whom Providence has placed at the pinnacle of the monarchy and our house [the emperor].

Sending you to Hungary has another purpose: that you can make yourself useful to your sovereign, the state, and the fatherland. Because you will occupy a post at the top of a respected military power, you must endeavor to learn the art of war, which is only suitable for princes of high birth. You must be able one day to serve effectively at the head of an army, should your sovereign so desire. *Therefore you must possess more merit and more knowledge than others. Your birth alone will not suffice; it could bring you only misfortune and disgrace.*

Since you have decided not to marry, you should concern yourself all the more eagerly with making your fortune, providing charity to all, serving the state, and earning for yourself undying fame. Some of your ancestors have achieved this goal, as have even private persons like Prince Eugene, Louis of Baden, Montecuccoli [all military figures in the late seventeenth and early eighteenth centuries], and others who have won immortality through their deeds. You can achieve such fame more easily than they because you have the advantages of your birth and your education; you need only the desire.

I hope that neither the pope nor your order insist that you take the holy vows. But as I wish that you not be required to take them, so I also wish even more emphatically that you follow them willingly and sincerely, as if you were bound. Allow yourself no indulgence; you are responsible for your salvation and to your calling. Do not be led astray by derision or bad examples which you have seen or heard. Reject all talk that is disrespectful of your elders or injurious to a young heart like yours. Never be ashamed to appear at every opportunity a good Christian in word and deed. This point demands the greatest exactness and attention, now more than ever, because morals have become all too corrupt and frivolous. People want to enclose religion in their hearts without practicing their faith openly because they fear they will be laughed at or called hypocritical and narrow-minded. This is the mood that now prevails everywhere, and which is all the more dangerous because everyone who considers himself part of the "beautiful world" accepts it and does the same as the so-called enlightened writers. Nothing is more pleasant, nothing more suitable to flatter our egos as a freedom without restrictions. "Freedom" is the word with which our enlightened century wants to replace religion. One condemns the whole past as a time of ignorance and prejudice, while knowing nothing of that past and very little of the present.

If I could see these so-called enlightened figures, these *philosophes,* more fortunate in their work and happier in their private lives, then I would accuse myself of bias, pride, prepossession, and obstinacy for not adjusting to them. But unfortunately daily experience teaches me the opposite. No one is weaker, no one more spiritless than these strong spirits; no one more servile, no one more despairing at the least misfortune as they. They are bad fathers, sons, husbands, ministers, generals, and citizens. And why? Because they lack substance. All of their philosophy, all of their axioms are conceived only in their egotism; the slightest disappointment crushes them beyond hope. The mass of these people—who are killing themselves—become insane or at least mentally incapacitated only as a result of their bad behavior or illness. And when God bestows his grace on a few of these wretches so that they return to the righteous path, it so happens that they, because of their uselessness to the state, retreat into some dark corner in order to hide from the eyes of the world. But such cases rarely occur; usually these people die after a highly stimulated life of debauchery and doubt. Such a calamity I can only beg you to avoid. You should follow strictly only that which you have learned in your youth and have observed until now at our court.

If you have seen and investigated the misery and pettiness of human life and feel perhaps an inclination to dedicate yourself to a spiritual career, you can do so only after your twenty-sixth birthday and with the approval of the head of your house, whom you must obey always in regard to your person. As I have advised you against selecting a spiritual career, which demands much virtue and piety and requires such great duties, so I also advise you against marriage, especially when I observe contemporary marriages. The position that I have chosen for you is the safest, most pleasant, and least dangerous, but you must have the sense to realize it. Without substance and without virtue, every career is precarious, dangerous, and unhappy.

Shun everything that involves passion, especially concerning women. Regrettably, I must say that they are more dangerous than the most dissolute men. If you fall once, you are lost. You will be able to redeem yourself only with difficulty; I know your character too well not to believe that. Scrupulously avoid the first step and be especially wary of any deception or wickedness which drags so much misfortune behind it; only the most debauched give themselves up to it.

Never be alone with women, either in a box at the theatre, during visits, or while taking walks. Be sure one of your aides accompanies you. Never entrust anything to the opposite sex, but treat women with great respect and courtesy, even those of bourgeois origin.

In ten years, my dear son, many things will appear completely different than they seem now. Then you will agree that your old mother has spoken the truth. A younger person, especially of your personality, needs someone who provides the truth and is intent on making life pleasant and worthwhile for him. But whereas nothing is more precious on earth than a true friend, so is one difficult to find. In general we find many who would like to be our friends, but we must choose them very carefully. The greater good luck it is to discover a true friend, the greater bad luck would it be, especially for you, to find false friends. For forty years I have known [Count Francis Xavier] Rosenberg, and generally he has served me well and has earned my trust. In the most painful, difficult situations he has endeavored to educate and sustain Leopold and his wife and to earn the reputation which he enjoys, of securing their happiness and the contentment of their lands. You know that the sensible, obvious course would be to live and treasure him, and that this was the result in the foreign countries where he represented us. Is that not overwhelming proof of his character and personal service? You must therefore obtain and follow his advice concerning everything. He is not difficult to please, and in this I do not have the same trust in him as in other things. He is all too indulgent, amiable in affairs, and full of natural courtesy. Nonetheless, I hope that he will impart to you these characteristics, which you completely lack. But to do so you must lay aside those prejudices that you have heard spoken against him, and you must obey him. I know his devotion; he will certainly soon love you if you show yourself obliging and confident even in the smallest things.

By expressing these opinions, I have striven to discuss and include the most important points which relate to your journey and your absence. If you will read them through sometime in the spirit of love and trust which you have shown to me thus far and which I, through my motherly concern, have earned from you, then you will find nothing therein that is irrelevant or difficult to follow. Whoever criticizes these views will consider them unnecessary and burdensome. I flatter myself with the hope that you will not think so, that you will follow them, and that you will sometimes read them with someone who enjoys your trust. My sincerest wishes go with you. If you follow my suggestions and do not stray from the path of virtue, then this trip will be pleasant and profitable. It will acquaint you with the world and with people. It will procure for you the esteem and approval of the people; that is no trifling affair for a young, late-born prince who is beginning his life. It would fill me with satisfaction if I were still living when you returned, for you would make my old age and long life more bearable. Should I not be here, however, I cannot repeat often enough that you obey the head of your house in everything, to serve him and the state willingly and eagerly, and to provide an example to others by your religious conviction, your flawless morals, and your devotion to your family.

God give you his grace and ordain that I hear much more good of you than of your brothers. I kiss you and give you my blessing.

HER DAUGHTERS

Maria Theresa also offered advice to her daughters, particularly on the subject of marriage and a wife's duty toward her husband. The following passage Maria Theresa wrote to her second oldest daughter, Maria Christine, her beloved "Mimi" who had inherited so many of the characteristics of Francis Stephen, on the occasion of her marriage to Duke Albert of Saxony-Teschen. Despite her frequent emphasis in this letter on the subordination of the wife to the husband, Maria Theresa herself never allowed her own spouse a decisive voice in affairs of state.[4]

You have asked that I give you advice concerning your future marriage. A number of books exist which deal with this problem,

[4] Maria Theresa to Maria Christine, April, 1766, in W. Fred, ed., *Briefe der Kaiserin Maria Theresia* (Munich and Leipzig: Georg Müller, 1914), I, 346–51. Translated by the editor.

but I will not repeat what they say. You know that we women are subject to our men, that we are obligated to be obedient to them, and that our single endeavor should be to serve our husband, be useful to him, and make him both a father and a best friend. Even though many examples seem to belie this view, I can by no means release you from your duty to follow it. You chose your husband because you loved him. That was the reason why I arranged the marriage for you. You know your husband, and you have every reason to hope that you will be as happy as one can be in this world.

Try to serve God through a Christian life. Be to others an example by your generosity, your piety, proper manner of living, and respectful modesty. You must set a correct tone for your entourage, and I am convinced that you are well adapted to do so.

You possess charm and devotion, but guard against exaggerating these virtues and attractive characteristics. I should emphasize that you, in your tender love for your husband, should not counsel him excessively, to the point that it becomes a burden to him. Nothing is so delicate as this little matter; the most tender and most virtuous women and those who marry for love often ruin their marriages on this point. You must also be sparing of your most innocent caresses; you must try to make him want and desire you. In our century one wants above all no restraints. . . . The more you allow your husband freedom, in which you ask for his tender attention with the least insistence, the more love-worthy you will become; he will demand you and surrender himself to you.

As your chief goal, you must be certain that he finds in you good humor, pleasantness, and kindness. Be sure to entertain and occupy him, so that he does not feel more comfortable elsewhere. In order to win his trust, you must serve him by your conduct and your discretion. Never should any suspicion enter your heart. The more freedom you allow your husband and the more you show him your feeling and confidence in this regard, the more attractive you will become to him. Every marital happiness consists of mutual trust and mutual kindness; passionate love vanishes quickly. Each must respect the other, and each must be useful to the other; each must feel true friendship for the other in order to be content in marriage, to bear the tribulations of this life, and to promote life's happiness. Such happiness must be your foremost goal. In this regard I fear you will incline to excess, which could influence somewhat your joy together. I have seen you jealous of your friends; guard against being jealous toward your husband—that will only serve to alienate him. Do not provoke him in this matter. Teasing leads to reproaches and then to bitterness; the mutual esteem and pleasantness of life vanish, and antipathy results. The more trust you show your husband and the less pressure you inflict upon him, the more securely you will tie him to you.

What good fortune for him to find in you a loving wife at home, a wife creating happiness for her husband, supporting him, comforting him, being useful to him, never presuming to afflict him, allowing him instead to come to her, being satisfied with his frequent visits, and finding herself happy when she can be occupied with him. If you do not realize this immediately, you will certainly suffer the consequences later on.

All marriages would be happy if people followed this advice. But everything depends on the wife, who should pursue the proper course, try to win the attention and trust of her husband, never abuse or boast of it, and never feel the desire to rule him. In this matter your situation is even more delicate than mine. Never allow him to sense your higher birth; nothing is difficult if one loves truly and sensibly. Of this I am certain.

Allow yourself no coquetry, no jealousy. Listen to no gossip. Show to gossipers that you are above such chatter. For a married woman, everything is important and nothing frivolous. Dress yourself modestly; married women cannot wear the same clothes as young girls, and, when you set the example, the others in your court will follow.

Have no confidants; your husband should be the only one, and I do not make myself an exception in order to get you into the habit of sending me confidential reports. You have enough spirit and talent, if you want to utilize it, to make yourself very happy; indeed all the more so, since more than anything else, the character and demeanor of your husband should comfort you in the future if you do not tarnish your fortunate situation.

You must try to occupy and to fascinate your husband; that is the only way not to be defeated by sluts. A man enjoys pleasure much more if he takes only moderate doses of it; you have seen enough examples to know that.

Order in your personal affairs and in your household is the key to a quiet and happy life. I know that in our time people believe no pleasure is possible if there is the slightest coercion. I cannot agree with this view because I personally have had the experience and I have daily observed that these same people who espouse this contention are the most bad tempered and the least happy. They enjoy nothing truly because they allow their caprice and senses such freedom that they eventually are ruled by them.

I speak of that discipline that unites your will with the will of your husband. You must stop at nothing to adjust yourself to him in all affairs, and you must sacrifice everything if it concerns pleasing him or doing his will. After you make your objections and suggestions full of gentleness and affectionate love, you have no alternative but to obey his decision. You may give your advice only once. If he decides otherwise, you can do nothing but agree in such a way that he sees that you do it happily, without thinking of some other method to change his mind. Nothing is easier, when you love sincerely and know your duty; in this world that is the only way to be contented and happy. When your husband sees you solicitous for his happiness through your kindness, and you constantly endeavor to make certain he is more contented, more satisfied, and more secure at home than elsewhere, then you can be certain that you will captivate him and provide a firm foundation for his and your happiness. But you must not want to force him to stay at home; he himself must be convinced of it.

Through their pleasantness and their skill, the ugliest and oldest women have repeatedly pleased and attracted people and aroused in them the strongest passions, while the prettiest women were ignored because they lacked these virtues. The less foolishness you display, the better it will be. That is another modern evil: it consists of a great emphasis upon spirit and the idea that people can play tricks on each other without impropriety. This tone also engenders indiscriminate confidence which produces a sharpness in social life and expels all decency and all civility. Allow at your court no two-faced talk and no malicious backbiting. Make this clear immediately, so you will keep evil elements at a distance. At every opportunity show your eagerness to maintain virtue. Dismiss from your company anyone who violates this principle. Be sure to observe all the servants at your court. Assume the responsibility for keeping your people in order. Do not examine them personally in this matter, but let them be reprimanded by their superiors, without you yourself taking part. That is the only way to be well served and to keep skilled people.

Here I have said nothing to you concerning your own behavior. Neglect none of your religious duties; in marriage prayer and God's help are even more necessary than in single life. Your spiritual lessons should occur regularly. I recommend very strongly that you be exact in this matter. Regularize your devotions as well as your moderate offerings according to your confessor's advice. . . .

The good Lord has conferred upon you many talents and advantages; He has undoubtedly selected you from your whole numerous family to be the joy and comfort of your parents and a righteous, clear-seeing sister-in-law; He has secured for you a virtuous, loveworthy husband of your own choice. I hope that this good Lord will complete His work and make you happy, assuming that you do not abandon Him and that you follow my advice, which will mislead you as little as my tender love. I give you my blessing, embrace you affectionately, and remain your devoted mother.

HER ELDEST SON AND HEIR, JOSEPH II

Of all the differences separating Maria Theresa and her eldest son, none was so fundamental as their disagreement over religion. Whereas Maria Theresa firmly believed in the necessity of maintaining the Roman Catholic faith, Joseph felt that toleration of all beliefs was essential to the stability of a modern state. In the following two letters, written in 1777 while Joseph traveled in western Europe, the empress expressed her own opinions on toleration in response to suggestions by Joseph that it would be beneficial to allow each man to worship as he pleased. These letters, by the way, had little impact on her son, for as soon as his mother died, he issued an edict of toleration, permitting Protestants, Greek Orthodox, and Jews to worship freely.[5]

No dominant religion? Toleration and indifference are truly the perfect means of undermining everything so that nothing can be sustained, and we will be most affected by it. It is not the Edict of Nantes [a French edict of 1598 granting Protestants political equality; it was revoked in 1685] that has ruined these lands because at Bordeaux no such edict has ever existed, and that country is no better off. The farming out of taxes, incompetent administration, and weak or corrupt ministers have ruined this otherwise well-situated land. The lack of religion among the civil servants, who concern themselves only with their personal interests and emotions, has

---

[5] Maria Theresa to Joseph II, n.d. and July 5, 1777, in Alfred von Arneth, ed., *Maria Theresia und Joseph II: Ihre Correspondenz* (Vienna: Carl Gerold's Sohn. 1867), II, 146–47, 157–59. Translated by the editor.

ruined everything. What limitations curb this kind of people? None, neither the gallows nor the rack, but only religion or cruelty. As the useful saying goes, *No friend of mankind is he who allows his people to think for themselves.*

I speak only of political necessity, not as a Christian; nothing is so necessary and useful as religion. Do you wish that each person create his own according to his fancy? Without an established faith and the supremacy of the Church, what will become of us? Tranquillity and contentment will certainly not result: as history shows us, the law of force and other evil consequences will follow. Just one word from you could ignite the greatest misfortune and render you answerable for the welfare of thousands of souls.

But think how I suffer when I see you immersed in these errors. At stake is not merely the welfare of the state, nor even your loyalty as a son who since birth has been the sole object of my actions, but your personal salvation. By observing, hearing, and mixing this spirit of contradiction with your desire to create, you are destroying yourself and dragging down with you the whole monarchy, which your ancestors have left to us after taking great pains to improve it and in which they have used great care to introduce our holy religion, not by force and cruelty like our enemies, but with care, concern, and at great expense. As long as I live, I will permit no persecution but also no toleration or indifference. I wish only to live until I can meet my ancestors with the conviction that my son will be as great and as religious as his predecessors; that he will reject his false ideas, evil books, and especially those who have sought to brighten their careers at the expense of all that is most holy and respectable and who want to introduce an imaginary freedom, which can never exist and which can only result in license and total degradation.

Pardon this long letter, this great digression. I love you and my lands too much not to become concerned. I regret that I can keep you only fifteen days, since I am so busy with plans and affairs of state. I am glad it is July, for this will be the last month I will not see you. I will be happy when you will at last remain in one spot; my personal faculties are beginning to fail me.

This is what you will find in Switzerland. The people there will not recognize the value of your presence. There in that asylum for all the debauched and criminal live a couple of our women whom I hope you will not see. They were sufficiently brazen to go there, and I must say, to my great chagrin, that there will be nothing more to ruin if you continue to think seriously about this general religious toleration, which you claim is your greatest principle. I hope—yes and I will not cease to pray and request others more worthy than I to pray—that God will preserve you from this illness, which will be the greatest the monarchy has ever suffered. By believing that through religious toleration you will encourage, protect, and even attract more farmers to our lands, you will instead ruin your state because you will cause so many souls to be lost. What good is it for you to follow the true faith, if you love it so little that you will do nothing to preserve and augment it? I do not see the Protestants so indifferent in these matters, just the opposite. In fact I hope we imitate them because no state can consent to an equality of faiths. You will observe this in that villainous Switzerland. There they accept and experiment daily with everything that comes from Germany, England, Saxony, Baden, Holland, etc.—with the exception of Prussia—but are they happy? Have they those farmers who are so necessary to make a state prosperous? There exists no country less happy or more backward than these lands. A state must have a firm faith and immutable laws: how do you expect to find or protect them?

HER YOUNGEST DAUGHTER, MARIE ANTOINETTE

Aside from Joseph II, Maria Theresa's most famous offspring was her youngest daughter, Marie Antoinette, wife of King Louis XVI of France and romantic victim of the French Revolution. Thrust into the rather difficult French court at the tender age of fifteen, she married a weak-willed man who because of a physical infirmity, could not consummate the marriage until seven years after the wedding. Consequently she tried to drown her difficulties and disappointments in a whirlpool of entertainments, frivolities, and gambling. As one might imagine, this behavior on the part of a daughter of such a rigid, duty-conscious moralist as Maria Theresa brought a flood of advice, pleadings, and scoldings from Vienna. The first selection comes from a letter written by Maria Theresa to her daughter in August, 1771, just a year after the marriage and three years before Marie Antoinette's husband became king. Although the empress warns the princess to offer friendship to the ruling party at court in general, she really means that her daughter should show kindness to Madame du Barry,

*at that time mistress of King Louis XV and a woman to whom
Marie Antoinette would not speak.*[6]

The courier departed a bit late this time. I have encountered
an abundance of delays, and I am beginning to grow old at a furious
pace, so that even in my work I need double the time I used to. I
have received your portrait done in pastels, and it resembles you
quite closely. It is the delight of the whole family; I have put it in
my study and have moved the other one to my bedroom, where I
work in the evening. So I have you always with me, before my eyes;
you always live deep in my heart.

I impatiently await your comments concerning that which Mercy
[Count Florimund Mercy d'Argenteau, Austrian ambassador to
France] told me, but I have seen that you postponed this conversation until after the departure of the courier. But what has reassured
me is Mercy's report that you have begun, on his advice, to treat
politely the ruling party at court and have addressed a few vague
niceties to them which have had a marvelous effect. I dwell no
longer on this point; Mercy is authorized to speak to you forthrightly. I am only pleased that you are so ready now to follow his
advice. I am always certain that you will be successful in anything
you undertake because the good Lord has given you a pleasant
personality, many charms, and natural kindness so that all hearts
will be open to you if you undertake anything. But I cannot hide
from you my irritation that I must continuously hear from many
quarters that you have abandoned the polite and attentive act of
saying something agreeable and pleasant to everyone and have instead begun making distinctions among people. I have heard that
you have fallen deeply into this habit and that some people blame
it on the Mesdames [daughters of Louis XV], who never know by
themselves how to gain attention or to win someone's confidence.
But worse than that are various reports that you ridicule and laugh
at people to their face. This will harm you infinitely—as it should
—and people will doubt the goodness of your heart. In order to
please five or six young ladies and cavaliers, you will lose everyone
else. My dear daughter, a princess simply cannot possess such a fault.
It attracts to you only courtesans, generally idle people and the least

---

[6] Maria Theresa to Marie Antoinette, August 17, 1771, in Alfred von Arneth,
ed., *Maria Theresia und Marie Antoinette: Ihr Briefwechsel* (Leipzig: K. F.
Köhler, 1866), 40–42. Translated by the editor.

estimable in the state, and it repels honest people who have no wish to subject themselves to ridicule or to be laughed at. In the end you will enjoy only evil company, who will drag you into vice slowly but surely. Some also mention that you do not honor the Germans, that you do not give justice to the true merits of this nation. If you overlook a little awkwardness in exterior appearance and conversation, you will find in this people much real talent and merit, which foreigners have often praised.

I sympathize with your embarrassment at having to refuse [Victor Francis] Broglie the request he made for his wife. I cannot deny that I respect him for showing so much zeal in that most critical situation in which I found myself after the battle of Prague. You should find the occasion to remark to him that I will always remember him. I was happy that [Marquis] Durfort had an audience with you; he deserved it because of his real qualities and because he had the good fortune to seal the union by your marriage. [Durfort negotiated Marie Antoinette's marriage.]

All that I have heard about your being together—you four young people—gives me pleasure. Your sister-in-law has done you no harm and poses no threat to you, but her character is more solid and she has more knowledge. You can only benefit from your association with her, and naturally you will have to spend many years together. You should become close to her, not only for your own good but also for the good of the state. The better you get along, the less people will gossip about you; but the slightest coldness between you will give them a field day, and you will experience only too severely the resulting unpleasantness that will affect your privacy and your contentment.

Mercy reported that the little note I sent pleased you very much, and that you made the most joyous and touching comments. You know what effect that had on me. Never spoil the source of tenderness and good will that you possess and never copy from others who, notwithstanding their personal merit, have never succeeded in public. They have never understood and have never had examples before them from which to learn, but for you it is natural and you have seen its marvelous effects. I hope that my constant repetitions do not bore you but convince you that I speak them because I want to see you happy and help you to avoid the pitfalls of youth.

In this second letter, composed in December, 1777, after Louis XVI had become king and four months after an opera-

tion to remove his infirmity, Maria Theresa warns her daugh-
ter to give up her frivolous ways and spend as much time as
possible with her husband. In light of the fate of Marie An-
toinette and Louis XVI—both were guillotined in 1793—
Maria Theresa's forebodings about their future assume a sinis-
ter aspect that she doubtless never envisioned.[7]

I expect all the couriers to bring bad news because they are so
late. I hope for bad weather so that the king does not tire himself
by hunting too much and so the queen will not gamble during the
evening and far into the night. It is bad for your health and beauty,
very bad to separate yourself from the king, and very bad for the
present and the future. You are not doing the duty that you owe to
your husband. That he is too good is no excuse; in fact it makes
you even more wrong, and I tremble for your future. Have no
illusions; gambling brings with it wicked company and unfortunate
consequences in every country in the world. It is universally true
that if one desires to win too much, he is always the loser. If one
plays honestly, he cannot hope to win in the long run. Therefore,
my dear daughter, I beg you: abandon this habit; this passion must
be completely uprooted. No one can better advise you than I, for
I was in the same situation. If I cannot convince you, I will one day
write to the king himself in order to save you from even greater
losses. I know too well the consequences of your habit, and you will
lose much prestige among the people and especially abroad, which
hurts me greatly because I love you so much.

[7] Maria Theresa to Marie Antoinette, December 5, 1777 in Arneth, ed., *Maria
Theresia und Marie Antoinette,* 225–26. Translated by the editor.

PART TWO

MARIA THERESA VIEWED BY HER CONTEMPORARIES

The following contemporary views of Maria Theresa are not divided into laudatory or hostile categories, but rather into the various periods of her reign. They begin with the first difficult years of the War of the Austrian Succession, pass through the first reform era and the titanic struggles of the Seven Years' War, and end with the long period of relative tranquillity that characterized the empress's last two decades of rule. These opinions, noted at various times and by various people, provide fascinating insights into the personality of this woman as the problems she faced changed and the years passed on.

5
Voltaire: The Brave Young Queen

The leading figure of the French Enlightenment Voltaire wrote not only essays and satire but history as well. In the following passage from his Short History of the Century of Louis XV, *he presents the famous story of Maria Theresa's appearance, infant son in her arms, before the Hungarian nobility in 1741 to beg their succor in the struggle against her numerous enemies. Although it is true that she did address the Hungarian nobility, her baby son was not present, and the Hungarians promised their support only after some hard-headed negotiations with Maria Theresa's ministers concerning the guarantee of certain wide-ranging Hungarian privileges. Nonetheless, the willingness of these nobles—who had a long tradition of antipathy toward the Habsburgs—to stand behind their sovereign in her hour of need and Maria The-*

resa's continued deference and frequent expressions of thanks
to them fortified this romantic legend and contributed greatly
to Maria Theresa's fame throughout Europe.[1]

Now France, Spain, Bavaria, and Saxony stirred themselves
to crown an emperor. Bavaria pressed France to procure for it at
least a portion of the Austrian succession. In his writings the
elector claimed the whole inheritance, but he dared not order his
ministers to ask for all of it. Therefore, Maria Theresa, wife of
the grand duke of Tuscany Francis of Lorraine, took possession of
all the domains left by her father; she received the homage of the
Estates of Austria at Vienna on November 7, 1740. The provinces of
Italy and Bohemia sent deputies to give their oath of loyalty to her.
She especially won the approval of the Hungarians by agreeing to
accept the venerable law of 1222 of King Andrew II, which read:
"If I or any of my successors, in whatever time it be, want to in-
fringe upon your privileges, then you will be allowed, by virtue of
this promise to you and your descendants, to defend yourselves
without being treated as rebels."

The more the ancestors of the queen-archduchess had shown
themselves adverse to enforcing such pledges, the more also this
prudent step—of which I will speak later—endeared this princess
to the Hungarians. These people, who had always wanted to shake
off the shackles of the house of Austria, embraced the yoke of Maria
Theresa; after two hundred years of sedition, hatred, and civil war,
they changed completely to a spirit of adoration. The queen was
crowned only a few months later at Pressburg [Bratislava], on June
24, 1741. She became not only a queen, but she entered all their
hearts with a popular affability that her ancestors had rarely exer-
cised; she banished that etiquette and arrogance that had made the
throne odious without making it more respectable. Her aunt the
archduchess, governess of the Low Countries, had never eaten with
anyone. Maria Theresa admitted to her table all the ladies and all
the officers of distinction. The deputies of the Estates spoke freely
to her; she never refused an audience, and no one left her discon-
tented. . . .

(September 11, 1741) The more the ruin of Maria Theresa appeared inevitable, the more courage she revealed; she had departed

[1] Voltaire, "Précis du siècle de Louis XV," in *Oeuvres complètes* (Paris: Garnier
frères, 1878), XV, 192–93. Translated by the editor.

from Vienna and threw herself into the arms of the Hungarians, treated so severely by her father and ancestors. Having assembled the four orders of the parliament at Pressburg, she appeared there holding in her arms her young son, barely out of the cradle. Speaking in Latin, a language in which she expressed herself well, she addressed them in words similar to the following: "Abandoned by my friends, persecuted by my enemies, attacked by my closest relatives, I have no other resources than your loyalty, your courage, and my steadfastness; I place in your hands the daughter and son of your king who rely on you for their safety." Pulling their swords from their scabbards, all the attending nobles and their friends cried out *"Moriamur pro rege nostro"* (We will die for our king Maria Theresa). They always give the title of king to their queen, and no princess has been more deserving of this title. They shed tears in declaring the oath to defend her; she alone retained her composure, but when she had retired with her women of honor, she allowed to fall in abundance those tears that her strength had held back. She was pregnant at that time, and shortly afterward she wrote to the duchess of Lorraine, her mother-in-law, "I did not even know if a village would remain to me where I could deliver my baby."

Under these circumstances, she excited the zeal of her Hungarians; she inspired England and Holland in her favor, and they gave her financial assistance. She won support within the [Holy Roman] Empire; she negotiated with the king of Sardinia, and his provinces gave her soldiers.

All the English nation responded in her favor. This people is not one that waits for the opinion of its master in order to express itself. Some people proposed to present a gift to this princess. The duchess of Marlborough, widow of the Marlborough who had fought for Charles VI, assembled the important ladies of London; they promised to furnish one hundred thousand pounds sterling, and the duchess herself deposited forty thousand. The queen of Hungary had the grandeur of soul not to accept this money that had so generously been offered to her; she wished only that which she received from the whole nation assembled in Parliament.

6
Charles VII: The Ruthless Enemy

Upon Maria Theresa's ascension to the Habsburg throne, Charles Albert, elector of Bavaria, realized the moment had come for him to fulfill his dream of annexing certain Habsburg lands and becoming Holy Roman emperor. Seizing the opportunity offered by the failure of the House of Habsburg to produce a male heir and by Frederick's victories over the Austrians in 1741, Charles forged alliances with France, Spain, and later Saxony. He then invaded Bohemia, captured Prague, and secured his election as emperor—the first non-Habsburg to assume that honor since 1438. His success was short-lived, however, for to his surprise, in January, 1742, the empress's army under Khevenhüller erased the Bavarian gains in Austria proper and soon occupied most of Bavaria itself. From then until his death in January, 1745, Charles Albert had to flee Munich twice again; he returned for the last time late in 1744 to die a disappointed man. In the first of the following selections from his diary, Charles reveals his deep chagrin and mild astonishment at learning of the Austrian offensive into his land just as he was celebrating his coronation as Holy Roman emperor. In the second, he expresses his agony at watching his patrimony oppressed while he lives in exile with what has become a worthless title.[1]

Finally after 11:00 P.M. Count Pappenheim, hereditary grand marshal of the empire, arrived with twenty-four postilions to bring me the news of my unanimous election as king of the Romans. I was immediately congratulated by all the court, and the day would have been perfect had my concerns about my country not troubled me. The next day my nephew, Duke Clement, ceremoniously brought me the election decree and the capitulation of the electoral

[1] Karl VII, *Tagebuch* (Munich: M. Riegersche Universitäts-Buchhandlung, 1883), pp. 47–48, 103–4. Translated by the editor.

college, which I received in a public audience so that I might accept it from an ambassador as distinguished as he was dear to me. The Elector Palatine ordered a Te Deum sung, and that evening sponsored a masked ball; from then on I was treated as Roman emperor. An enormous crowd gathered there [at the ball] and among the most noted guests was Prince William of Hesse, who offered me his compliments; on all occasions this prince showed a friendship truly as distinguished as his whole house.

I would have considered myself at the zenith of my ambition had not the bad news, sent from Linz by an aide-de-camp of Count Minuzi, filled me with great anguish. He informed me of the sad state of the French and Bavarian corps besieged in that town, which had had to surrender on the day of my election. This was not all; the town of Passau had been taken, the commander of the place allowing himself to be intimidated so that he gave up and promised to withdraw the garrison to Straubing. At Linz the officers submitted to the ignominious condition of not serving for a year against Maria Theresa, the French being obliged to retire to Donauwürth to proceed from there to France and the Bavarians being assigned to a place in the Palatinate to be interned for the remainder of the stipulated term. This catastrophe appeared all the more serious because not a single adequate corps remained to oppose the superior forces of Khevenhüller's army which numbered more than 20,000 men, and I suffered in seeing Bavaria inundated by its enemies. The taking of Passau and Scharding completely exposed the country, and I heard that another corps was menacing us from the direction of the Tyrol. The total ruin of Bavaria appeared inevitable, and I could envision no way to save it. As Khevenhüller's army advanced along the great road towards Braunau, ours was forced to withdraw. They occupied Braunau, as well as Burghausen, and inflicted extreme desolation on all Bavaria. In spite of all this I had to assume a happy countenance and prepare for my entry into Frankfurt, where everyone awaited me with much joy.

This retreat [withdrawal of the Austrian armies across the Rhine to take up winter quarters in Bavaria], disgraceful for these braggarts who have found conquest without resistance so easy, was the greatest misfortune for poor Bavaria. These troops, after forcing the inhabitants to utter an oath of fidelity and obedience in order to protect their lives, treated my subjects with a barbarism unparalleled among Christian peoples. This army has taken up winter quarters there and has exacted such a large amount of contributions and taxes that the people are obliged to surrender their goods in order to save themselves. It is in this manner that my Bavarians, who have so often delivered the Austrians from the invasions of the Turks, find themselves repaid by ingratitude. What a sad spectacle for me, who, though installed on the imperial throne, must be the spectator of the calamities of my states, without the power to save them.

7
Goethe: The Victorious Wife

*One of the great moments in Maria Theresa's life
was the coronation, in 1745, of her husband, Francis Stephen,
as Holy Roman emperor. For her this achievement symbolized
the first permanent victory over the ring of enemies that had
tried to deprive her of her inheritance at the beginning of her
reign. In this selection from his autobiography, the great German writer Goethe recounts an anecdote of Francis's coronation in the city of Frankfurt told by older people who, along
with him, had witnessed the coronation of Joseph as king of
Rome in 1764.*[1]

Older persons, who were present at the coronation of Francis
the First, related that Maria Theresa, beautiful beyond measure,
had looked on this solemnity from a balcony window of the Frauen-
stein house, close to the Römer. As her consort returned from the
cathedral in his strange costume, and seemed to her, so to speak,
like a ghost of Charlemagne, he had, as if in jest, raised both his
hands, and shown her the imperial globe, the sceptre, and the curi-
ous gloves, at which she had broken out into immoderate laughter,
which served for the great delight and edification of the crowd,
which was thus honored with a sight of the good and natural matri-
monial understanding between the most exalted couple of Christen-
dom. But when the Empress, to greet her consort, waved her hand-
kerchief, and even shouted a loud *vivat* to him, the enthusiasm and
exultation of the people was raised to the highest, so that there was
no end to the cheers of joy.

[1] Goethe, *Truth and Fiction* (Boston: Estes and Lauriat, 1883), p. 166.

8
Podewils: The Practical Ruler

In April, 1746, Count Otto Christopher Podewils became the first Prussian envoy to the court of Vienna since the outbreak of the War of the Austrian Succession. His function was not to engage in political intrigue but to observe the court and gather as much information as possible about its members, particularly the empress. Although he began fairly well, as the following excerpt shows, he found himself unable to extract information of great significance because he represented a recent enemy. This failure, plus poor health, a growing dislike of his job, and Podewils's contraction of enormous debts that Frederick had to pay, contributed to his dismissal in late 1750 and soon after his retirement to his estate. Nonetheless, in January, 1747, he did provide an excellent portrait of Maria Theresa, her appearance, habits, ambitions, likes, and dislikes.[1]

As ordered by Your Majesty, I hereby provide the characteristics of the most important personages of the court, as I have observed them.

I am not so conceited as to believe that the impressions I send you will be completely correct. It requires greater insight than I, as I know, possess. Furthermore, the condition in which I find myself [a recent enemy of Austria] forms an almost insurmountable barrier to acquiring a complete knowledge of the personalities of those individuals whom I have undertaken to describe. . . .

I begin with a portrait of the empress-queen, as the principal subject of my painting.

She is somewhat over medium height. Before her marriage, she was very beautiful, but the numerous births she has endured [at this time she had borne six daughters and two sons] have left her quite

[1] Count Otto Christopher Podewils to Frederick II, King of Prussia, in Carl Hinrichs, ed., *Friedrich der Grosse und Maria Theresia: Diplomatische Berichte von Otto Christoph Graf von Podewils* (Berlin: R.v. Deckers Verlag, G. Schenk, 1937), pp. 38–54. Reprinted, and translated by the editor, by permission of the publisher.

heavy. Nonetheless, she has a sprightly gait and a majestic bearing. Her appearance is pleasant, although she spoils it by the way she dresses, particularly by wearing the small English crinolines, which she likes.

She has a round, full face and a bold forehead. Her pronounced eyebrows are, like her hair, blond without any touch of red. Her eyes are large, bright, and at the same time full of gentleness, all accented by their light-blue color. Her nose is small, neither hooked nor turned up, the mouth a little large, but still pretty, the teeth white, the smile pleasant, the neck and throat well formed, and the arms and hands beautiful. She still retains her nice complexion, although she devotes little time to it. She has much color. Her expression is open and bright, her conversation friendly and charming. No one can deny that she is a lovely person.

When she became ruler, she knew the secret of winning everyone's love and admiration. Her sex, her beauty, and her misfortune helped in no small measure. The exaltations of praise issued in abundance by the officially subsidized journalists were believed by all. By showing only her good side—innocent, generous, charitable, popular, courageous, and noble—she quickly won the hearts of her subjects and convinced them that, as she had believed from the beginning, the late Emperor Charles VII was a criminal. She granted everyone an audience; personally read petitions; concerned herself with the administration of justice; accepted willingly the chores of government; rewarded one person with a kind word, another with a smile or courteous sign; made her negative replies bearable; gave splendid promises; and publicly displayed the greatest piety, remarking often that she would trust everything to God. She honored the clergy, displayed much reverence for religion, expressed her love for the poor, founded hospitals, divided money among the soldiers, sponsored ceremonies, allowed plays to run, and personally addressed the landed Estates, to whom she described in exalted and moving terms her situation and bewailed the misfortune into which her enemies had thrust her. She called herself disconsolate to be forced against her will to share her calamities with her loyal subjects and promised at the first opportunity to reward the ardor of each. She promised the Hungarians to reestablish and confirm their old privileges and told them she wanted to remedy their old grievances. She publicly displayed her spiritual strength, showed defiance to her misfortune, and tried to instill her own courage into her subjects.

I heard only words of praise for this empress. People extolled her to the clouds. Everyone considered himself fortunate. The landed Estates paid to her all that they could. The people bore their taxes without murmuring. The nobility offered her money, often without waiting to be asked. The Hungarians insisted they would fight for her; the officers served happily for half-pay because she had convinced them that it was not her fault she could not give them more. Full of enthusiasm, everyone stood by her and rushed to sacrifice himself for this best of all princesses. People deified her. Everybody wanted to have her picture. She never appeared in public without being greeted with applause.

A more pleasant personality was hard to imagine. Perhaps it would have been less difficult to acquire it than to display it in public. The queen could do so only a short time. Misfortune increases her delight in being loved and increases her desire to be loved. The reversals which she suffered at the beginning of her reign brought out this desire, but the success of her policies after the Treaty of Breslau [1742] reduced it somewhat. Slowly but surely, however, she has again assumed her natural character. The effort to hide her spirit under the veil of misfortune has now disappeared. I begin to notice that she, less motivated by the difficulties of her people than by the thought of increasing her power, prosecutes the war without aversion [Although at peace with Prussia, Austria was still at war with France]. The exaltations which everyone had showered upon her, and her own egotism have given her a high opinion of her talent and her ability, and have made her domineering. She listens to advice only grudgingly, allows no contradiction, tries to arouse fear rather than love, fancies herself as proud as her ancestors, treats many with arrogance, and shows herself vengeful and intransigent. She hears impatiently the petitions brought to her, tries to encroach upon the privileges of the Hungarians, oppresses the Protestants by relieving almost none of their grievances, and gives a bad impression of her piety, in which she displays so little respect for religion that one day she went to church on a horse, prompting the clergy to decry such an act as a great scandal and to voice their public disapproval.

So great a change in her character elicited considerable reaction among her subjects who began to protest the taxes they had to pay and expressed great discontent over them. They no longer wished to see her on the streets or to possess her picture. Almost everyone believed he had grounds for complaint.

Nevertheless, I must add: much else contributed to the general unhappiness. It was impossible for the queen to satisfy everyone, to keep all the promises she had made, and to fulfill in every case the high opinion which she had given of her personality and talents. The more complete the good fortune that each one promised himself during her reign, the more he believed he had reason to complain that his expectations were not realized.

One can also not deny: if the queen does not possess all the qualities that she at first displayed to a degree that won for her the admiration of all, she still deserves great praise. She apparently recognized the damage she had done to herself and tried to correct it, although I doubt if she will again be as popular as she once was.

Her spirit is lively, masterful, and capable of dealing with affairs of state. She possesses an excellent memory and good judgment. She has such good control of herself that it is very difficult to judge from her appearance and behavior what she really thinks.

Her conversation is almost always friendly and gracious, and displays the coyest courage. Her behavior is easy and captivating, and appears even more so to her subjects, who are accustomed to regarding pride and arrogance as qualities inseparable from their monarchs. She speaks well, expresses herself gracefully, and appears to listen attentively. It is still easy to gain an audience with her, although somewhat less so than at the beginning of her reign, when anyone could speak with her. In order to win an audience now, we must go to the court lady who supervises the calendar. Seldom has the empress refused one, however; she listens with patience and good will to those who address her and personally replies to the petitions that reach her. On days at home she spends the greater part of the time, whenever she has the chance, in granting audiences. When she is in the city, the same thing happens while everyone attends court. In the garden she usually grants audiences while walking. She gives almost no audiences in circumstances where one is displeased. A short time ago she had told a Hungarian general who had requested an audience that she would see him the next day during a reception. He heatedly replied that he had no wish to be seen and scrutinized by everyone, and, if she was not willing to see him in private, as the dead emperor and she herself had done earlier, then he would rather not see her at all. At first she was quite enraged, but necessity demanded that she grant his wish.

She spends a great deal of time with affairs of state and seems to have an excellent knowledge of them. She reads most of the reports from her ambassadors at foreign courts or has them read to her, examines the rough drafts of important documents before they are written in final form, converses often with her ministers, and attends the conferences which concern state business of some magnitude. Above all she wants to be thoroughly instructed about matters concerning the army. She tries with some success to penetrate the personalities and talents of the generals. She herself chose all of those who served in the last Italian campaign, and everyone agreed they were the best of her officers.

Her ambition cherishes the wish to rule personally. She enjoys more success at it than most of her ancestors, but the personal interests of her ministers and her court inspire them to prevent or hinder her from having an exact knowledge of her business, so that she will not remedy those abuses of which they and their families take so much advantage. This resistance makes her efforts, if not completely useless, for the most part unfruitful. She knows people deceive her, but she can do nothing about it. Often she expresses her impatience and has more than once said that she wishes God would open her eyes to the corruption in the government.

Nonetheless, she has ended many abuses and cut unnecessary expenses. She plans to undertake still more reforms in finances and the army, and concerning both, she suggests to her ministers Your Majesty's system as a model. She sometimes shows them the remarkable difference between the revenues which Your Majesty extracts from Silesia and those which she and her ancestors received, and refuses to accept their excuses that this province is being oppressed.

She also envisions one day reordering the condition of the army, especially establishing its wages on the same system as Your Majesty's. It is unlikely, however, that she will ever succeed. The generals and ministers have too many interests not to oppose these changes, and they do so by creating insurmountable obstacles and difficulties in her path. Only those officers who have no connections would gain advantages from a regularizing of wages. But those who have influence at court, either themselves or through their parents, would continue to receive far greater rewards in the disorder that now prevails.

In order to forestall these reforms, the ministers and generals have already posed a thousand difficulties regarding even the minimal changes the empress wants to introduce. I recall that, one day when she stopped a regiment during a parade, she commented that she found their overcoats too long and suggested that they must be troublesome to soldiers during marches in great heat or rain. She added that they should change to the Prussian model. Instantly the officers argued that the troops needed these long coats to cover them at night, whereas the Prussians did not need them because every

Prussian tent had blankets. She replied that each of her soldiers should have a blanket too. The next day she received an estimate of the cost. Someone had so exaggerated the expense for the blankets, the packhorses to carry them, and the people to care for them, that the total came to an enormous sum, which easily convinced the empress to abandon the idea.

She tries to praise the military, which now enjoys greater respect than under the late emperor. Repeatedly she has said that under her reign a man could make his fortune with his dagger only. She allows officers in her service to eat at her table regardless of their birth. Such a policy greatly displeases the high nobility, which is already quite offended that the empress has abolished many traditional court practices that in general she hates passionately.

She goes to some lengths to win the soldiers by her generosity, often permitting money to be divided among them and seldom passing by the life guards without giving them a few ducats. By doing so she has become beloved by the troops, whose admiration she has also won by the determination she has demonstrated during the most serious defeats. It is certain that she has intended for a long time to assume command of the army herself.

She especially tries to belie the weaknesses of her sex and to strive for virtues which are least suitable to her and which few women possess. She even seems angry to have been born a woman. She spends little time caring for her beauty; she exposes herself without consideration to the vagaries of the weather, strolls many hours in the sun and in the cold, which she tolerates much better than heat. She cares little about her attire and, aside from ceremonial days, dresses very simply, as does the whole court now after her example.

One could never accuse her of coquetry. In this respect, she has never given one hint of infidelity. She loves the emperor dearly, but also demands great devotion from him. People claim that her love for this prince is caused partly by her temperament and the good qualities with which he can satisfy it. Among other things they emphasize the little influence which he, despite her love for him, has on her spirit. I have it on good authority that one day during a conference in which the empress had heatedly defended a position against the views of her ministers, she in very sharp words told the emperor, as he made known his opinion, that he should not mix in business he did not understand. The emperor grumbled about this treatment for a few days and complained about it to one of his favorites, a Lorraine colonel by the name of Rosières. This man answered, "Sire, permit me to say that you have handled the empress the wrong way. Had I been in your position, I would have forced her to treat me better, and I would have received her as limp as a glove." "Why should I?" asked the emperor. "I wouldn't be able to sleep," answered the colonel. "Believe me, she loves you in this way, and by refusing her, you could achieve everything." This conversation was reported to the empress, who hounded this officer so unmercifully that he decided to leave the service, despite all the emperor's efforts to get him to stay.

Without doubt she is very jealous of the emperor and does everything possible to prevent him from establishing a liaison. To the few women whom the emperor had begun to notice, she has thrown very grim looks. She would like to forbid all gallantry at her court, and shows great contempt for women who have love affairs and just as much for the men who court them. I know that one day she had a vehement argument with Count Esterhazy—for whom, incidentally, she has much respect and who always attends her card parties —concerning a love affair that he has openly enjoyed with the wife of Count Althann. She tries to keep the emperor from everyone inclined to such adventures, and people say that Count [Rudolph Joseph] Colloredo, who makes no secret of his liaisons, will never win her good will. For some time he has been in a form of disgrace because he took the emperor on a few pleasure trips. The same thing has happened to a few others. She wants to live a middle-class marriage with the emperor.

She dearly loves her children, who are always around her on holidays. She used to love the oldest archduchess [Archduchess Elizabeth who died in June, 1740, at the age of three] the most, but she has died. Now she prefers Archduke Joseph. She lets him get into many things for which she must reprimand him. Sometimes she assumes an appearance of strictness toward him and vows not to spoil him. One day she wanted to have him whipped. Someone remonstrated with her that there was no precedent for anyone acting in such a way towards an archduke. "I believe it," she replied, "and look at how they turned out." She loves her mother very much but allows her no participation in affairs of government.

She enjoys entertainment, without depending on it too much. Earlier she had more love for dances and masked balls than now. She dances with enthusiasm and, for her figure, with agility. She loves gambling and plays cards quite boldly but appears sensitive about it. Once she lost more than one hundred thousand ducats. It was rumored that Sir [Thomas] Robinson [the British ambassador] received orders from his court to reproach her for it.

Although she plays the harpsichord, and that quite well, and apparently understands much about music, she makes very little of it.

One of her greatest pleasures is to go for walks and, above all, to ride horseback. She rides fearfully fast. The emperor and others have tried vainly to slow her down. She first learned to ride in preparation for the Hungarian coronation. She believed it politically sound because she had noticed that the Hungarians expressed much enthusiasm upon seeing her on horseback. She discovered such fervent pleasure in this recreation that it has become her fondest enjoyment. Sometimes she rides on an estate, at other times to private houses to eat breakfast or drink coffee. She also goes on many walks, sometimes three to four hours at a time.

She seldom hunts and does so only to please the emperor.

She loves architecture, without understanding it very well, as her house in Schönbrunn, built according to her taste, testifies.

By nature she is happy, but it appears that the disappointments she has had to bear have embittered her, and now she is somewhat harsh. Apparently she has taken her misfortunes extraordinarily to heart, and one day I heard her say that she would not begin her life over again for anything in the world.

People call her fickle, and it is certain that her favorites do not enjoy their positions long. Countess Fuchs and her daughters, Countesses Logier and Daun, have generally stood out, but all three, especially the mother, were more than once on the verge of seeing their favor disappear had not the emperor troubled to reconcile them with the empress. They have, after all, little influence and even then only indirectly and in roundabout ways. The only person most noticeably in favor is one of her chamber ladies called Fritz [Elisabeth von Fritz]; Maria Theresa just married her to a Hungarian nobleman named Petrach, to whom she has given a present of twelve thousand gulden and appointed to the bodyguards with the rank of lieutenant colonel. People say that this woman, who still attends the empress, offers her advice even on affairs of state. I have doubts about this last rumor because it accords neither with the spirit of the empress to rule by her own will and to see and do everything personally, nor with her care to eliminate the slightest doubt that she herself rules.

The empress has never renounced her own generosity. She is by nature benevolent and likes to make everyone happy. She makes a little too much of her gratitude and displays it openly at frequent opportunities.

Her habits are well ordered. In the winter she rises at 6:00 A.M.,

in the summer at 4:00 or 5:00 and devotes the whole morning to
affairs of state, reading reports, signing documents, and attending
conferences. She eats lunch around 1:00 P.M., rarely spending more
than a half an hour at the table. Often she eats alone. In summer
and even sometimes in winter she goes for a walk after lunch, often
alone, and spends most of the rest of the afternoon reading reports.
From 7:00 to 8:30 P.M. she usually plays faro. In the evening she
eats little, most often only a broth, sometimes goes for a walk after
dinner, and usually goes to bed before 10:00 P.M.

She takes little medicine, relying instead upon her healthy constitution. When she feels hot, even in the middle of winter, she often
sits at an open window in the room in which she eats, which annoys
everyone but herself. Her doctors repeatedly tell her that she will
regret this practice, but she only laughs at them.

Her method of judging affairs of state I have already had the
honor of presenting to Your Majesty in my regular reports. She
possesses extraordinary ambition and would like to make the house
of Austria more glorious than it was under her ancestors.

She has had the joy of reaching one of her ambitious goals, the
return of the imperial crown to her house.

She seems to have inherited from her ancestors the traditional
hatred of France, with whom, I believe, she will never have good
relations, although she has sufficiently mastered her passions, should
her interests demand it.

She does not like Your Majesty, but she respects you. She will be
unable to forget the loss of Silesia, which grieves her all the more,
I hear from good sources, because at the same time her troops lost
their honor. In general, she regards Your Majesty as a hindrance to
the growth of her power and above all to her influence in the [Holy
Roman] Empire, which she would like to expand as did her ancestors.

These are, Majesty, the main points which I have been able to
collect regarding the personality of the queen-empress. I intend to
send to Your Majesty the portraits of the other members of the
court, as soon as my business permits me. I beg Your Majesty's pardon in advance if I do not reply to your orders as quickly as I would
like. Because I personally cipher and decipher all messages in the
interests of greater security, Your Majesty will realize that I have
little leisure time left to me.

9

Khevenhüller: Disturber of the Old Order

During his many years of service as Maria Theresa's master of the household, Count John Joseph Khevenhüller composed a voluminous diary, stretching over the period from 1742 to 1776 and containing day-by-day comments on virtually every aspect of court life in Vienna. A scion of an old aristocratic family, Khevenhüller took a dim view of Maria Theresa's reforms, which he believed threatened the advantages enjoyed under the old system by his class. In this somewhat chaotic diary entry, Khevenhüller expresses his discontent at the changes, wonders how the new jobs will be distributed, and worries that this "Prussianization" of Austria is fostering the decline of his own class and the emergence of a lower order of "pencil pushers." [1]

On May 2 [1749] the empress signed the authorizations and memoranda concerning the new important internal reforms. Although their details have largely been kept secret—as is the case in most such matters—I have learned a few things about them. Because no one is really certain of how the new system will succeed, everyone is much more anxious to learn its contents. It is known that the Bohemian and Austrian chancellories will be combined into one office, the court martial court and governorship in Prague abolished, and the government divided into two branches, thereby overthrowing the whole administrative and judicial system that has endured for centuries. Everyone appears affected by these changes; in fact, each seems all the more depressed because no one expected such a revolution. After its implementation everyone fears that even more reforms will be contemplated because, once the spirit of innovation

[1] Johann Josef Khevenhüller-Metsch, *Aus der Zeit Maria Theresias* (Vienna: Adolf Holzhausen, 1908), II, 318–22. Translated by the editor.

begins to reign, it is not only difficult to suppress but expands ever wider until it eventually spreads confusion everywhere.

The empress, however, may have had a much less pessimistic impression. This woman has been overrun with so many complaints about the administration of justice, especially the frequent struggles among the various courts, that she finally decided to separate judicial affairs from regular political and public affairs. In order to end the preference shown by the chancellories for their own lands, she will create out of the erstwhile Bohemian and Austrian high courts a combined supreme court and will place this court exclusively in charge of justice so that provincial preference will not distract it from the speedy due process of law.

After achieving this goal last August by the creation of a court commission under the direction of Count Haugwitz and having it confirmed by the court deputations meeting in the presence of both their majesties, she quite naturally carried her changes further and, after abolition of the chancellories, established this court commission as the highest authority in administrative affairs. Its title will be the General Directory (according to the Prussian example, which undoubtedly serves as the model for this whole new creation).

Because the public has exaggerated and glossed over much of the details and has gossiped, unmindful of the noble purposes (as I believe) of those changes introduced by the empress, I find it necessary to examine the printed documents published in the newspapers and the so-called Vienna journals. On the basis of a written recommendation to the empress and emperor from my brother-in-law (in which he recommended strengthening the authority of the empress in legal matters), a few modifications will alter the court martial court, and —in order to preserve the preeminence of the sovereign as final judge—the government will probably approve the following: (1) that the sovereign's legal procedures must be kept separate from the ordinary judicial channels and (2) that they be assigned to the president of the General Directory and to the secretary of the court martial court, Dr. Hertl von Hardenburg (whom the empress tried to appoint to the supreme judiciary but who declined), who will be assisted by another official.

Despite these and other amendments and modifications in the main project—which, on the empress's express order, were drawn up by Cabinet Secretary Koch, Government Chancellor Mannagetta, and Bohemian Court Chancellor Kannegiesser (all dependable) and in which were included articles and passages partly of a special nature and partly openly opposed to the recognized and affirmed Estate prerogatives—the empress did not have the good fortune of quieting the outburst of feeling that erupted at the introduction of such extensive reforms. Instead of the thanks that she expected from the public for a more moderate and speedier course of justice, everyone complained of even greater confusion, and up till now it does not appear that anyone predicts a better course of things in the future.

Meanwhile the chiefs of bureaus, after receiving their orders to prepare to depart their offices, did not fail to notify their subordinates. Both lord chancellors (Counts Harrach and [John Frederick] Seilern) initiated the procedure, and Harrach, who is quite a natural orator, said goodbye in such moving phrases that almost all around him cried; he, who also appeared close to tears, cut his speech short and locked himself in his office (to let his tears flow). At the government building, owing to the absence of a governor (Count Kueff-stein, the governor, upon learning of the new changes, resigned his post a few days ago after securing a yearly pension of 4,000 gulden), the vice-governor, Count Breuner, had to supervise the dissolution and read aloud the list of those who will be assigned to one or the other of the new governmental divisions. My son-in-law (who, after receiving dispensation from the provincial laws, had joined the administration only shortly before last Easter vacation) has been allotted a position in the judicial branch.

At the same time everyone is trying to find out who will be the new heads. To Count Harrach the empress had offered the choice of either presidency of the new supreme judiciary or the first position in the old *Deputationsrat,* now called the Conference for Internal Affairs. He chose the latter, receiving a supreme chancellor's salary of 36,000 gulden, and authorization to cosign all public edicts with Count Haugwitz (Haugwitz sent the protocols to Harrach not so much for advice as for inspection), which means that he has the honor of posing as prime minister for domestic affairs.

The supreme presidency in judicial affairs was given to Count Seilern, who wanted to possess the title of chancellor; to please him, the empress awarded him the rank of chancellor of supreme justice. Both Counts Oed and Kortzensky remained vice-chancellors. Haugwitz gained the presidency of the General Directory. Count Losy became president of the administration *in publicis,* so reports have to go immediately to the Conference for Internal Affairs. Although Count Haugwitz does not exclusively receive and act on all of these reports, he seems to have enormous influence in all the channels of the supreme directory. Count Breuner holds the presidential role in judicial affairs but is subordinated to the supreme judiciary, where appeals originally sent to the chancellory must now go. The rooms in the old Hofburg assigned in the past to the Lower Austrian administration will be used from now on by Count Haugwitz and his directory, and the new justice department must set up its quarters in the *Vicedom* bureau.

Count Losy holds meetings in his house, and, owing to the year-long renovation of the magistrate building, will have to continue to do so. Consequently he has taken the staff list into his charge, and Count Breuner—when he undertakes the publication of the discharge papers—has to borrow it from him.

What matters and responsibilities will be the charge of each department is set forth specifically in the pieces concerning the present new system. Because the reported enclosures contain the most essential decisions, I have not speculated further about them, but rather want to conclude that I wish that those who continue to speak with the empress in this matter do so with pure intentions. They cannot possibly sanction the way the work has gone so far. If they are truly loyal, they will wish that Her Majesty will consider such a work— which has as its object the entire overthrow and recreation of a form of government grown customary from the beginning and through many centuries of this most illustrious house—not on the advice of a few insignificant pencil pushers, but with the consultation of her ministers and those other honorable persons who possess noble sentiments and are interested in her true glory. And there is no place here for the hesitations of these same project makers (namely, the whole reform would get bogged down) because either the objections proposed by other honest and wise people are important or they are not, and a ruler as enlightened as our empress can quickly judge the difference. If they are not important, she will not be led astray from her good intentions; if they are, however, she must reconsider the situation so she will not have to return to it regretfully later (to the detriment of her prestige) and undo what has happened after much irreparable harm has occurred.

10

Fürst: The Successful Reformer

Despite Podewils's skepticism and Khevenhüller's concern, Maria Theresa's reforms were put into effect, and the results were not long in forthcoming. Among the observers of their success was Charles Joseph Maximilian Fürst und Kupferberg, a Prussian official assigned to Vienna in 1752 to regularize commercial and tariff affairs between Prussia and Austria. Young, alert, and particularly interested in the Austrian reforms, Fürst composed his observations on the implementation, which he published in a small work entitled Lettres sur Vienne écrites en 1755.[1]

The empress–queen enjoys the reputation of having established her finances on a better footing than they were on under her ancestors. The frightful expenses occasioned by eight years of war, the debts that upon her succession she found crushing her country (at the time her father's treasury held only twenty thousand gulden), and the loss of the greater portion of Silesia required her to consider a totally new financial structure as soon as the war ended. During the war itself, the court seemed concerned only with luxuries, parties, and lavishness, so much so that the English were justified when they complained that the Austrians used their subsidies for the wrong purposes. But after the peace, everything changed. Income has increased, expenses have been cut; debts are paid and no new ones contracted; the army is stronger and well financed; all salaries are paid, and efforts are made to accumulate surplus funds for future needs.

Count Haugwitz deserves the credit for this achievement; he did

[1] Reprinted from Leopold von Ranke, *Zur Geschichte von Österreich und Preussen zwischen den Friedenschlüssen zu Aachen und Hubertusberg*, Vol. XXX of *Sämmtliche Werke* (Leipzig; Verlag von Duncker und Humblot, 1875), pp. 20–26. Translated by the editor.

not create this system by himself, but for the most part, he brought it to fruition.

Now I will talk about the reforms, which he gave to the government.

Earlier special chancellories existed for Italy, Hungary, Bohemia, and its adjacent provinces, and for Upper, Inner, and the western Austrian lands.

Count Haugwitz began by uniting the Bohemian and Austrian chancellories, and then introduced the following divisions within it. For judicial affairs a supreme court was created, while all other matters were referred to the great General Directory, whose president Haugwitz became. The empress appointed him supreme chancellor of Bohemia and first chancellor of Austria.

He introduced the same separation of powers in the provincial bureaucracy. To the local government he left only judicial matters, and for everything else he created financial bodies under the name of representations. These offices are assigned to the administration and, most important, the finances of the provinces under the authority of the Directory. The most able personnel were then appointed.

One can see, especially by the names, that the General Directory in Berlin served as the model for this creation. Whereas the imitation is clear, the reform does go much further: it has more completely removed the justice department and has attached to every representation a member with judicial authority, from whom one can appeal only to the General Directory, where a commission makes the final decisions.

Under Haugwitz serve Count John Chotek as chancellor and Baron Bartenstein, the erstwhile state secretary. The administrators in the chancellory are divided, according to custom, into two classes, the counts and lords, and the knights and scholars. Among the latter are a number of quite capable individuals.

The course of business is most convenient for the members. On Wednesday the new business is divided among the councilors. By Friday they must have it prepared for presentation. On Monday is the great session, in which they make reports, and often on that day they work at the office until 8:00 in the evening. On Tuesday Count Haugwitz presents the reports on these matters to the empress, who promptly makes her decisions. By the next Monday the chancellory has to have all the edicts implemented. Even with this routine, the officials of the Directory still enjoy many free days.

When this Directory was created, Count Haugwitz's first concern was to place the income of his princess on a firm foundation in order to maintain and finance a respectable military establishment during times of peace.

The personal lands of the empress are of no consequence. The princes of the house of Austria were never good economists and gave most of them away, especially to the church. In Austria and Moravia there are almost none left; in Bohemia they are in the hands of the emperor, who has paid off the mortgages which encumbered them. Only the Hungarian lands remain, which can yield a million gulden profit.

Given these conditions, most of the state income comes from the contributions [from the Estates].

Earlier the custom was that the Estates were asked to grant a specific number of soldiers and amount of money. They never wanted to grant as much as requested, so the government had to demand more than it expected to receive, and even then the Estates gathered their contributions very slowly. All these elements made administration very difficult and uncertain, and the government could not function expeditiously. In 1747 Count Haugwitz suggested an agreement with the Bohemian and Austrian Estates, by which they promised to pay a specific sum over a ten-year period and in exchange should be relieved of certain, previous obligations. The main point is that all payments, rations, forage, horses, transportation facilities, and so forth were estimated and affixed to a specific sum. The empress promised not to raise the contributions in those ten years, but to try to reduce them. Only now the Estates must pay much more overall than earlier. Bohemia paid 3,200,000 gulden in 1731, 5,270,-488 in 1754. Lower Austria 900,000 in 1731, 2,008,960 in 1754; Styria 390,000 in 1731, 1,182,545 in 1754. In 1731 the contributions, including those of Serbia and Silesia, totaled 12,420,000 gulden; now, even without those provinces, they total 16,897,856.

People complained—especially in the Austrian lands—not only about the rise in taxes but also about the inequalities of their allotment.

In each province rectification commissions were named through the Estates in order to equalize assessments. A commissioner with four assistants—two clerks and two economists—travels through each province in order to evaluate the provincial revenue on which the contribution is based. Naturally that procedure takes very long and requires much expense. Each commission receives thirty-two gulden daily, which amounts to 75,920 gulden a year. Although these officials are forbidden to receive gifts from any influential parties or to eat with them, I have personally seen some dine very well at the table of Count Wilzek zu Sebern. The economists, who execute the appraisals and whom the commissioner oversees but must rely upon for his reports, are pleasant people who have made bankruptcy their business.

In each major city of the province there exists a deputation of the Estates, to which the commissioners report and to which a few members of the representation are attached. These deputations are in turn subordinated to the rectification-court commission, which forms a part of the Directory. The most important man in this commission is a certain Spiersch from Silesia, formerly the chief accountant in the newly created Prussian domain board, whom Haugwitz seduced and attracted to Vienna, even though the man has remained a Lutheran. The president is Count Potstazki, earlier one of the most vigorous aides of Haugwitz, but whom the enemies of this minister now wish to set against him. He has little self-reliance, and the general respect that he received earlier when he came to Vienna, he no longer enjoys.

In general the contributions themselves are collected with great diligence. No one is exempt, lay or clerical. Every circle has a tax collector, whom everyone must pay every three months; each province has its general office to which the tax collectors bring their collections every three months. Whoever fails to pay on time is assigned a 10 percent interest charge by the chief tax collector of the Estate; it begins on the day he failed to pay. As the principal and interest of the delinquent taxes steadily approach the value of the property assessed, the individual often proceeds to sell that property publicly to pay the sum. The nobility must answer for their serfs and make good the same laws against them.

11

Frederick the Great: The Worthy Opponent

In 1756, after the reforms had been instituted, Maria Theresa felt the time had come to again take up the struggle for possession of Silesia. Once more her adversary was Frederick of Prussia, a ruler who discerned and appreciated in Maria Theresa a talent and determination equal to his own. Around 1763 Frederick wrote a history of the Seven Years' War; in it he discussed with some gusto the preparations made by himself and the empress for the renewal of their conflict.[1]

In 1755 the king [Frederick II sometimes refers to himself in the third person] augmented the regiments of the garrisons: those of Silesia were increased by eight, those of Prussia by three, those of Brandenburg by two; that made thirty battalions in all. In a poor country a sovereign does not find his resources in the bank accounts of his subjects, and his duty is to cover extraordinary but necessary expenses by his prudence and good economy. Supplies collected in the summer are consumed during the winter. It is just as necessary to use our funds economically in peace as it is in war. This point, unfortunately so important, was not forgotten, and Prussia was prepared to conduct a few campaigns with its own funds; in one word, we were ready to enter the arena at the first moment and to test our steel with the enemy's. In the following you will see how useful was this precaution, and why the king found it necessary, by the unusual situation of his provinces, to be armed and ready for all possibilities in order not to serve as a plaything for his country's neighbors and enemies. On the contrary, it was possible to win victories, if the resources of the state permitted it.

The king had in the person of the empress-queen an ambitious and vindictive enemy, even more dangerous because she was a

---

[1] Frederick the Great, *Histoire de la guerre de sept ans* (Berlin: Rudolph v. Decker, 1847), I, 7–9. Translated by the editor.

woman, obstinate in her opinions and implacable. This was so true that, in the secrecy of her dressing room, the empress-queen prepared the grand projects that burst forth later on. This superb woman, devoured by ambition, wanted to travel all roads gloriously; she put her finances into an order unknown to her ancestors and not only utilized reforms to make up for the revenues lost when she ceded lands to the king of Prussia and king of Sardinia, but actually increased her overall income. Count Haugwitz became controller-general of finances, and under his administration income rose to 36 million gulden or 48 million écus. Her father, Emperor Charles VI, who had even possessed the kingdom of Naples, Serbia, and Silesia, never received that much. Her husband, the emperor, who dared not interfere in affairs of state, threw himself into business ventures; each year he extracted enormous sums from his revenues in Tuscany and invested them in commerce. He established manufacturing companies, lent money, supervised the delivery of uniforms, arms, horses, and weapons for the entire imperial army. Associated with a Count Bolza and a merchant named Schimmelmann, he won the contract to farm the taxes of Saxony and in 1756 even provided the forage and flour to the army of the king of Prussia, who was engaged in war with his wife, the empress. During the war the emperor advanced considerable sums to this princess as good credit: in short, he was the banker of the court, and in character with his title of king of Jerusalem, he conformed to the immemorial profession of the Jewish nation.

In preceding wars the empress had sensed the need of improving discipline in her army. She chose generals who were both hard working and capable of introducing discipline among the troops. She also put old officers, little able to do their proper jobs, on pensions and replaced them with young men, who were full of enthusiasm and love for the business of war. The empress herself appeared frequently in the camps of Prague and Olomouc in order to inspire the troops by her presence and gifts. Better than any other prince, she knew how to use those distinctive flatteries which subjects love so much. She rewarded those officers who were recommended by their generals, and above all she excited their devotion, talents, and desire to please her. At the same time she formed a school of artillery under the direction of Prince Liechtenstein; he increased this corps to six battalions, and utilized cannon to a degree unprecedented in our day. Because of his ardor for the empress, he contributed 100,000 écus to the school out of his own pocket. Finally, in order to neglect nothing that would improve the military, the empress founded near Vienna a college to instruct the young nobility in the arts of war; it includes able professors of geometry, fortification, geography, and history, which constitute the appropriate subjects. This school serves as a seedbed of officers for her army. Owing to all these efforts, the military in this country has achieved a degree of perfection it had never reached under the emperors of the house of Austria, and it was a woman who realized the plans worthy of a great man.

This princess, little satisfied with the manner in which foreign and domestic affairs were treated and able to impress her opinions on all areas of administration, selected Count Kaunitz to serve her at the end of 1755. She awarded him the office of first minister so that his one head could encompass all the branches of government. We have had the opportunity to become especially acquainted with this man who plays such an important role. He possesses all the sentiments of his sovereign, and he knows how to flatter her passions and win her confidence. As soon as he entered the ministry, he worked to create that alliance system that would isolate the king of Prussia and prepare the way for the empress to achieve her dearest ambitions: the conquest of Silesia and the humiliation of the Prussian monarch. But that is the proper story of the following chapters, so we will not speak further of it here.

That is how these two powers used the peace to prepare for war —like two wrestlers flexing their muscles and burning with desire to grapple with each other.

Upon hearing the news of Maria Theresa's death, Frederick the Great, himself sixty-eight years old at the time, wrote a brief letter to a friend in which, after philosophizing a bit on death in general, he paid the highest compliment he could to his worthy rival.[2]

For my part I am becoming increasingly apathetic, a condition to which age leads the senile chatterer. Without becoming dis-

[2] Frederick II to Jean le Rond d'Alembert, January 6, 1781, in Frederick the Great, *Oeuvres* (Berlin: Rudolph v. Decker, 1854), XXV, 171. Translated by the editor.

turbed, I see dying and being born as dependent on when the command comes for one to enter the world or leave it. In this way I accepted the death of the empress-queen. She did honor to her throne and to her sex: I fought wars with her, but never was I her enemy.

12
Kaunitz: Preserver of Peace

After the Seven Years' War, the idea of reconquering Silesia no longer obsessed Maria Theresa. She had fought two major wars without having achieved its reconquest and had no wish to fight any more. In the following selection from one of his own testaments, Count Kaunitz explains how the formidable alliance between France and Austria—originally forged to wrest Silesia from Frederick—will henceforth be used to preserve the peace of Europe.[1]

Observations concerning the present foreign policy of the Viennese court, 27 September, 1764.

The foreign policy of the Austrian government consists of three major parts: (*a*) The universal, concerning all European courts and involving general international affairs; (*b*) the special, notably the German Empire, its internal constitution, and its security; and (*c*) the particular, namely the trusted understanding with Mainz and other patriotic imperial bodies.

Concerning the universal: (1) As its fundamental principle the Habsburg court vows to maintain the prevailing defensive alliance and understanding with the House of Bourbon, especially with France, as long as this house fulfills the duties of friendship and unity and does not compel the court of Vienna to assume unusual obligations. This alliance is based on mutual self-interest which, upon closer examination of present world conditions, appears quite natural; without doubt, this accord will lead not to a weak but to a lasting and self-perpetuating state system.

The most important reasons for maintaining it include the following: (*a*) Before the alliance with France and after Silesia fell into Prussian hands, all the Habsburg crownlands were exposed to constant and obvious danger. Prussia threatened the heart of the mon-

[1] Prince Wenzel Kaunitz-Rettberg, "Denkschriften," *Archiv für österreichische Geschichte*, XLVIII (1872), 63–68. Translated by the editor.

archy; the Ottoman Empire threatened the kingdom of Hungary; France, the Netherlands and the German Empire; and Spain and Naples, the Italian possessions and Tuscany.

(b) With the outbreak of the last war [the War of the Austrian Succession] this situation became even more dangerous and alarming because France was associated in one way or another—good relations, defensive alliances, or subsidy treaties—with Prussia, Denmark, Sweden, Naples, Cologne, Bavaria, the Palatinate, Braunschweig, Hesse-Cassel, Anspach, Bayreuth, Württemberg, and considerable other imperial bodies, so it could have drawn such a number of powerful enemies around the neck of the House of Habsburg that we could have expected aid from virtually no one. All that remained were Holland and England, but neither seemed a reliable friend.

(c) For instance, Holland had virtually withdrawn from the European balance of power.

(d) England would have directed its whole political attention only at France and would have cared little about its allies on the Continent.

(e) Therefore we could never have expected effective support from England against Prussia.

(f) In fact, England would have favored much more the electoral house of Brandenburg [Prussia] and would have wanted to make it the leading anti-French power on the Continent—to the detriment of the House of Habsburg. Proof of this policy was revealed in the last war, when England wanted to burden Austria with the whole responsibility and danger of fighting on land. Moreover, by negotiating and then initially signing the Treaty of Aix-la-Chapelle, England made certain all the signees would guarantee to Prussia the possession of Silesia and Glatz without guaranteeing to the House of Austria even the observance of the Treaties of Dresden and Breslau.

(g) In imperial affairs we could lose no more because Prussia had established itself as anti-Austrian and enjoyed the full support of France and all its purchased friends.

(h) The obtrusive dogmas and presumptions of the Protestants had risen to new heights; concurrently France had assumed the traditional policy—held since the Treaty of Westphalia—of keeping imperial authority and the House of Habsburg in constant embarrassment and danger by encouraging the Protestants. We had no other allies but the seapowers and Hanover, who, however, used the slightest excuse to refuse even the most minimal request of the Austrian government when it concerned the welfare of the Catholic religion in the empire. They argued that they could never approve any measures against their fellow Protestants, nor forfeit their trust and cooperation in political affairs. In this way not only did Vienna lose its few allies in religious affairs, but one of the most powerful Catholic crowns joined with the Protestants in supporting the same policies. Meanwhile, Austria experienced only defeats on all sides and could erect no limits to this spreading harm.

(*i*) The Austrian union with France has suddenly changed this unfortunate state of affairs for the better. Instead of many enemies as previously, Austria now faces only two potentially dangerous neighbors: the king of Prussia and the Ottoman Empire. No longer will Austria have to divide its forces, as was required by the last Prussian aggression, but can bring them from distant lands to defend the heart of the monarchy and even to attack the above-mentioned king. Above all else, this matter is most important. . . .

(*k*) Previously the [Austrian] Netherlands and the Italian possessions were regarded as distant lands, whose defense involved and weakened the House of Habsburg in the most difficult wars. Only in the last war did they become main pillars of the whole monarchy, not only supporting troops largely for the protection of the German crownlands but also providing financial gifts, surplus payments to the war chest, and loans of many million gulden in ready money. Another obvious example of the importance of the French alliance is the cancellation of the English subsidies, always so difficult to collect and yet never exceeding three hundred thousand to four hundred thousand pounds.

(*l*) Not to be overlooked in matters of imperial authority, the condition of the imperial constitution and Catholic religion have substantially improved under this new system, largely because France no longer bitterly intrigues against Austrian might or protests in the interest of Protestantism, but has obviously changed these traditional state policies. Since the time of Charles V, France took vigorous pains to deprive the Habsburgs of their imperial crown and to erect the greatest obstacles to each new election. The recent election of Joseph as king of Rome, which went so smoothly, was the first in which the French fomented no agitation.

(*m*) Another consideration is that since Prussia has so greatly increased its own strength and diminished Austria's through the conquest of Silesia and Glatz, Vienna could not provide its previous support to the crown of England even if it wanted to because, at the first declaration of war, France would occupy the Netherlands, hoping, as happened at the Treaty of Aix-la-Chapelle, to recover its losses in America. England would then commit the most unspeakable crime of state: it would leave Austria helpless against Prussia, thereby indirectly contributing the most to Prussia's steadily increasing enrichment. England would receive the support of 100,000 Austrian men against France in exchange for a paltry few hundred thousand pounds in subsidies. At the same time Austria and Prussia would have to employ their full resources for their own defense.

(*n*) But the Austro-French accord must be considered as a true system of peace. It must be preserved so that all courts which have no wish to fish in troubled waters may hope that the continuation of this accord will guarantee the general tranquillity and each state's individual security. Neither Austrian nor French interests can view with equanimity either one's attempt to enlarge itself or to tip the balance of power in its favor. Furthermore, no one needs to fear a German war against France, and the king of Prussia himself will be less inclined to break the peace because he must now worry about French support for the Austrian court. At the same time, these other states need not fear an increase in Austrian influence in the empire because France will not allow it.

(*o*) As its second principle of state, the royal imperial court has adopted general peace and good relations with all powers, including the king of Prussia, as long as he avoids any offensive alliance treaties against Austria and restrains from fomenting any unrest. It is also noteworthy that the existing rumor that the court of Vienna has joined the so-called Franco-Spanish family compact and has erected a triple alliance with these two crowns is completely without foundation. Until now, only Spanish accession to the Franco-Austrian defensive treaty of 1756 has been suggested, but it is still not in effect and could remain incomplete.

(*p*) Austria focuses its greatest attention on the internal strengthening of its lands through improvements in culture, manufacture, commerce, and finance. Also it concerns itself with its numerous peacetime military forces, which—including the troops stationed in Hungary, the Netherlands, and Italy, the border troops, and the retired soldiers—number a little over 200,000 men. This army entails considerable expense, which cannot be covered in subsidy promises or other offerings of money.

(*q*) Austria will maintain good relations with its neighbors and carefully avoid anything that could worry them. Although we will treat all other powers with restraint and reasonableness, we will remain ready to undertake resolute measures should necessity demand it. The conclusion then is that, except for the king of Prussia and the republic of Venice, good relations exist with the Ottoman Empire, Poland, and all our other neighbors, and all seem satisfied with this sincere Austrian friendship.

13

Joseph: The Difficult Coregent

Upon the death of her husband in 1765, Maria Theresa had her heir, Joseph II, crowned emperor and elevated to the office of coregent. Unlike his father, Joseph was not content to stand aside and dabble in affairs that interested the empress only slightly. Arrogant, ambitious, and convinced that his mother's reforms were haphazard and inadequate, Joseph constantly sought to impress upon her his own conviction that immediate, extensive, and thoroughgoing change was essential to preserve and strengthen the monarchy. Usually Maria Theresa listened attentively to Joseph's advice, but she did not follow it wholesale; in fact, she rarely followed it because she regarded his recommendations as entirely too liberal and his innovations as too severe. These fundamental differences between Joseph and Maria Theresa caused a great deal of animosity, argument, and exasperation between them—the son periodically offering to resign and the mother either volunteering (in an ocean of tears) to abdicate or telling Joseph to mind his own business. In the following excerpt from one of his letters to his mother, Joseph complains not of her rejection of his suggestions but of her failure to either reject or accept them. The reader should note the subservient tone of the letter and Joseph's use of the third person to refer to his mother.[1]

Although this morning I had the opportunity to converse frankly and openly with Your Majesty, I nonetheless would consider myself derelict in my duty if I did not repeat in writing what I said earlier and thereby provide authentic proof of my sincere and honest sentiments, which she can use as she believes best for her service and her serenity.

Long before today (as Your Majesty will recall), I predicted the almost insurmountable difficulties rising from the post Your Majesty

---

[1] Joseph II to Maria Theresa, December 9, 1773, in Alfred von Arneth, ed., *Maria Theresia und Joseph II: Ihre Correspondenz* (Vienna: Carl Gerold's Sohn, 1867), II, 23–27. Translated by the editor.

has given me. She and God are my witnesses that I foresaw these troubles from the moment she declared that my office of coregent would not be simply an empty title. All the bitterness, my prayers then that I have repeated since, and, finally, my conduct have confirmed my views. I have realized that, given my situation and perhaps my way of thinking, I cannot enjoy the role of my late august father. What have I done? I have tried to travel in order to remove myself from the precious intimacy of Your Majesty's tenderness. I have emphasized my distinction in my signature; I have searched for laxity; and finally I have judged carefully every idea as if I owed it to the spirit of Your Majesty. I know well that people may try to abuse me and that two wills are not always able to agree perfectly but must create some uncertainty and open the way to cabals, intrigues, and factions.

These principles I have always followed, and if I dare say so, it is only Your Majesty whom I have had to combat. She, because of scrupulousness, disgust, restraint, and little confidence in my ideas, has often done all that is imaginable to make me forget who I am and to make men doubt my status. If I have often revealed my precautions, and if, in having her honor, her service, and her tranquillity in mind, I have done some deed to displease her, then I very humbly beg her pardon; my good intentions must be my excuse. Knowing that the immense machinery of the government of the monarchy does not function as it should, I only conceal from her items that appear irrelevant. It is useless for her to examine here and there trivial events and their background. But because she allows me to do nothing alone if it was begun by us both, even though I am full of confidence in her good will, I think that we do not do that which our situation demands.

What am I? I never cease to ask myself that question and I hope that I have not forgotten who she is. And what is she doing with me? Her good will has blinded her to the first question and her taste to the second. She thinks I am everything except that which I want to be and am able to be. If she believes me ambitious or anxious to rule, she does not do me justice. I would have a great heart if I did not fear the future. This is true; God is my witness. She misjudges my ability if she believes me so full of talent and genius as to be capable of directing the most important affairs. I am proving to be only remotely honorable, of a lazy nature, hardly studious, shallow, and thoughtless. I must say to my shame that I am more froth than substance and must add that, aside from my zeal and uprightness in questions of the well-being of the state and its service, nothing is entirely stable in my person. But in affairs of state I am trustworthy.

My opinions, my advice, are those of one of her servants who have no right to give them except when she asks for or demands them. She should not base her decision on anything except convincing arguments, and she must decide without appeal. And we must express to her our thoughts without any consideration except what we believe best for the state. I can swear to her that I have always followed this path, but if she will permit me to say it, often it is she who has not wanted to make a decision and has neither adopted nor rejected the different opinions she has received. If the excuse she gives for acting this way is lack of confidence in herself, it is unjust because I can tell her without flattery—which does not enter into this letter—that she has never acted wrongly when she has acted by herself. If she claims divided advice as her excuse, she is wrong because she is much too intelligent to confuse my inexperience with the reputations, talents, and resources of other ministers who have for so many years earned the confidence of Your Majesty and the rest of the world.

If she is afraid to hurt me, if she believes that she must accept my opinion in some way, I only want the assurance that I stand irreproachable vis-à-vis myself; her rejection of my ideas, I assure her, will cause me no pain. But if she asks me for them, she must allow my convictions and my intellect to be my only guides.

In order not to bore her further with sentiment, of which she sees the effects daily, I ask that, for the good of the state, for her tranquillity, for my well-being, and for the well-being of all those who esteem her, she grant one favor: that she consider me and all her ministers as her councilors and servants and that we exist for no other reason than to ask for and execute her orders. That is our single, unique duty. All that is done in anything whatsoever, must come from her. She alone must be the common center, from which all must come and to which all must go. As we can have only opinions but no will, so she can have only will but no opinions. She herself can sense what confusion there would be if anyone even thought of telling her that he did something against her will, knowledge, or orders or informed her that she could not interfere in a certain department. If the people she has now, including myself, for some reason do not serve satisfactorily, she must change them. If I, because of my birth, because of the rights that nature and good fortune gave me more to her heart than to the realm, should be inconvenient to her or that she might find it dangerous to ask my opinions or inopportune to employ me, if my personage repels men one hundred times more useful and capable, then she should grant me in the name of God and her reputation, of her duty and tenderness, the retirement I wish.

None of my predecessors, contemporaries, or colleagues who are heirs presumptive are employed; why should I be? I desire nothing else than that she leave me to my affairs of the empire, to my books and honorable amusements. And why should she deprive me of the sweet life I would lead in this way, throw me prematurely into all the affairs of government, and allow me the cruel and frightful doubt that perhaps it is my own evilness which renders me an odious life and occupies me with the most disagreeable affairs? Does it make me the instrument and cause of the pains of Your Majesty, of confusion, disorder, malcontentment, disgust, and perhaps the loss of her ministers? In this world I love only her and the state; when she decides, she acts! If I would think only of myself, I know well what I would do! I am subservient to her orders for life.

14
Leopold: The Aging Sovereign

Maria Theresa's ninth child and third son was Leo-
pold, grand duke of Tuscany, who succeeded his brother,
Joseph, as emperor in 1790 and, after a quite successful but
unfortunately brief reign, died in 1792. In the following ex-
cerpt from an essay on the state of the family, composed for
his own use in 1778–79, Leopold provides an account of the
aging Maria Theresa and the people around her. Although
undoubtedly somewhat prejudiced by his position in and his
feelings toward the rest of the family, he nonetheless offers a
sharply critical examination of the empress and her increasing
inclinations toward pettiness, timidity, and trifling vindictive-
ness.[1]

Under present circumstances, the empress's health is to some
extent better than could be expected, although in light of her age
and her increasing corpulence, she walks with greater difficulty. As
soon as she takes a few steps or exercises in any way, she suddenly
begins to breathe heavily, and ashamed of it, tries to go very quickly,
which only harms her disposition and her morale. Her memory has
declined quite a bit; she does not remember many things anymore
and frequently repeats orders already given, thereby only generating
confusion. She has become a little deaf, and her constant ill humor
has restricted her courage and activity; she delays all business, and
in her household, her family, and affairs of state, lets almost everyone do what he wishes because she herself is constantly occupied
with prayer and devotions. She has her scruples about many things
and incessantly mistrusts herself and everyone else. Nothing makes
her happy, and she always appears lonely and melancholic, never
having visitors and always annoyed with everything.
    She is very depressed and disillusioned to see that all of the mat-

[1] Adam Wandruszka, *Leopold II* (Vienna and Munich: Herold Verlag, 1965),
I, 334–42. Reprinted, and translated by the editor, by permission of the publisher.

ters that she has struggled with for so many years have not been completed, that the public blames her for it, and that many complain about her. Almost constantly she laments over the land, the people, morals, and education, and expresses regret that her good intentions were not supported and that she will lose her spiritual well-being. She implies that she will completely remove herself from ruling because she now realizes that she is defeated and is a burden to everyone. I think, however, that she will never retire or abandon her realm.

Most of all she loves the emperor and knows no greater happiness than to see him praised and applauded; nevertheless, she likes to give him orders, guide him, and know everything that he has done or might do. She is especially sensitive to the way that he behaves toward her, and fears that he might openly degrade and belittle everything that she loves. She feels that he constantly criticizes and complains about all that she does or has done.

When they are together, there is unbroken strife and constant argument. If the emperor undertakes an act, affair, or order without telling her of it, she becomes very ill over it, especially if it is only a little thing. And if he does something either without telling her beforehand or bringing it to her attention, or does something that damages him in the eyes of the public, she is completely distraught. She may forgive him in everything, and it grieves her to the extreme if he does not appear a greater man than she would like to have him be. But then if she hears him praised in an affair of state, she is very jealous toward him, especially because she realizes the great respect that he enjoys among the people and knows that many people complain to him about her and say that if he ruled, everything would be better. She moans very much about that now and says that she wants to resign, that she sees that people can wait no longer for her to step down, and other such things. She entertains all doubts and suspicions that no one can tolerate her anymore, and that all stand by the emperor and follow him in order to win personal advantages and leave her in the lurch. All her complaints are trivial.

She harbors the greatest jealousy against anyone who speaks with the emperor, praises him, or writes to him for fear that that person will join the emperor against her. She always argues with him, even in the smallest affairs; they are never of the same opinion and fight with each other constantly over matters worth nothing. These trivialities generate more ill will than important affairs do.

In affairs of state, although the empress still retains great authority over everything, she is disheartened, does little, and follows anything anyone suggests to her almost without paying attention. In
this point she has become very lax and lets everything slide by. She
takes interest only in a few church or school matters, the creation
of a post or indemnity for someone, the construction in the garden
of Schönbrunn, or the appointments, gifts, and pensions from her
private purse. She listens to all her ministers but has no confidence
in them; she leaves them alone and does not interfere in state business. Especially in military affairs, which she gave over completely
to the emperor, she does nothing. She would like to mix in them
frequently in order to distribute favors and promotions, but because
the emperor will not defer to her, she is generally unsuccessful and
only troubles herself constantly about it. There are persons who, in
order to make themselves attractive to her, bring gossip about her
from the emperor or from various people, and such small talk causes
her more concern than do large issues. She has become very weak
and has lost her courage and fortitude. She has scruples about everything, experiences constant torment, wants always to be alone, and
complains to everyone about the emperor and her fate. Except for
Sundays, she grants only a few public audiences, but every hour she
sees ministers and officials. In general she spends much time in
church and in prayer and much time alone with her chamber ladies;
she always eats alone, and these women mean much to her. . . .

She is very happy to listen to news, especially that concerning the
emperor, and she allows herself to be won easily by those servants
who commiserate, sympathize, and agree with her. In this way, these
people gain influence in state policy. Because the empress trusts
none of the ministers, especially if she has been prejudiced against
them, she questions subordinate officials and appoints such under-
lings to important posts in all departments, which leads to confusing
and contradictory decisions and unexpected regulations. To them
she reveals everything and complains about everyone—even the emperor. She entrusts all business to them, even her letters, and they
in turn spread around the information she gives them, making themselves important with it, boasting of themselves, and putting their
knowledge to ill use. The emperor then hears about it, and painful
quarrels are the result.

Those who now push themselves upon her in church affairs in
particular and all policy in general include Cardinal [Christopher
Anthony] Migazzi, who, although she does not admire him and

knows him for what he is, still has influence and advises her as to her scruples; Bishop Kerens, a thoroughly crafty man who is in agreement with the cardinal and the Jesuit party; the prelate Dorothea, her confessor, a smart man but a Jansenist who alienates everyone; the prelates of Braunau, and Felbinger of Pressburg for school affairs, the latter a fraud and intriguer; the father Gratian of the Piarists and the rector of the Theresianum; the court chancellor Count Blümegen; the secretary Pichler; and Prince [George Adam] Starhemberg, who is in Flanders. She wants Starhemberg to be allowed to return, but the emperor cannot tolerate him, so he is seldom here. Also included are Count Rosenberg, who was recommended to her by Maria, [her daughter, Maria Christine] and to whom she pays court and confesses everything. Every morning he must come to her so that the empress can reveal and entrust everything to him. This group also numbers Count Lanthieri and the advisers Greiner and Kiemaier, the first of the Bohemian chancellory and the other of the deputation and commission for the academies, etc. and the court, both hated greatly in public; for police matters the secretary Carriere and Kap from the Department for Manufacture.

These people are always around, seeing, knowing, and doing everything; and this angers everyone else. Nonetheless, concerning business the empress consults no one but them. She always arises early, prays, and reads, and around eight o'clock she receives us, Maria Christine, and Maximilian until nine; then she hears two Masses, after which she gives audiences and sees people and ministers until noon. She always eats alone, then takes a short nap, after which she receives people until 6 P.M. Then she either reads or receives one or two officials, and around nine she goes to bed. Often, however, she gets up in the night and goes to work at her desk.

She almost never ventures into public anymore, receives no friends, never shows herself, and goes out only to visit a church or a monastery or to pray at the Capuchin church [site of the Habsburg burial vaults] on appropriate anniversaries.

She is interested in the small problems of private persons in order to bestow favors or to grant appointments, but in important affairs and in state business she almost never does anything except if someone suggests something.

She concerns herself but little with problems in Naples, and it appears that if someone speaks to her about them, she confides them to her heart and refuses to interfere. But she is a little annoyed with the queen [the queen of Naples was her daughter, Maria Caroline] and allows others to mix in her affairs.

She is especially angry with Parma [the duchess of Parma was her daughter, Maria Amalia], wants to hear nothing more about it, and mingles no longer either directly or indirectly in its business. She is also quite disgusted at France and the queen [Marie Antoinette] because the queen scarcely writes more than a few short notes. She also does not meddle with her because she regards the queen as corrupted and sacrificed [to state interests], but she is angry about the little attention the king shows her. She talks a bit more about Naples because Maria Christine always speaks of it and praises the king and queen before her.

For Ferdinand in Milan she holds a thoroughly inflated fondness and, although she complains a great deal about him and knows all his weaknesses, she sympathizes with him in spite of it. She explains everything to him, yields to him and supports him in everything, does everything for him so that he does what he wants. She believes all he says, and always declares wrong anyone who might oppose him. She tells him about everything, and he does with it what he wishes, even in the most unbelievable ways. His wife is just like him. Although the empress sees through her and even says so, this woman knows how to capture her with ceremony, calculated letters, and compliments. Consequently, she obtains everything she wants from the empress and misuses her influence abundantly in order to inflict much injustice and harm on many people. She is informed of everything that happens in Vienna by the Hardegg couple, her conscientious correspondents.

The empress frequently forgets what she has written or said to one person or another and so frequently writes or reports the same thing to someone else, thus bringing these people into some embarrassment when she good naturedly relates something that someone else had said about them. Often this can lead to painful confrontations with the emperor. Moreover, in her letters she complains strongly about the emperor to many people, and, as she retains no copy, these letters are often preserved among people who misuse them. By and large her papers are in no order and are open to the discretion of all, especially her chamber ladies, who often come into the room and seize the opportunity to read them. Consequently, everyone knows everything prematurely, especially the contents of those letters that she gives her ladies to seal and which they read. All these women are wooed constantly by those who serve foreign ambassadors, and to make things worse, none displays judgment or discretion in transmitting the empress's correspondence.

Frequently the empress gives an order to one department and then, out of mistrust, gives a contradictory order to someone else or commands a subaltern to advise her regarding the papers and attitudes of his superiors. Through the blunders of the chamber ladies, these orders often end up in the hands of the emperor or of persons who should not see them. The result is damaging misunderstandings for the whole civil service.

All of these incidents, as well as the differences in opinions between her and the emperor in almost all affairs, are generally known; in fact, both often speak of them. Consequently, among the officials and in all classes of persons there are people who say that they belong either to the party of the emperor or to that of the empress and subscribe to or will subscribe to one or the other for this or that reason. Such intrigue has an ill effect on these people as well as on the foreign ambassadors; it greatly damages state business and demoralizes everyone.

The empress has always displayed much good will and attentiveness for us, but she doesn't trust me. Because I do not run after her the whole day and pester her with compliments and acts of concern —which she likes—she thinks I have a taciturn personality. She regards my wife as weak and dominated completely by me and believes she would not venture to do or say anything without my telling her. Consequently, she doesn't confide in my wife and loves much more the one in Milan [Ferdinand's wife, Maria Beatrice], who pays her a wealth of compliments and lots of attention. She especially suspects that I am a devoted friend and follower of the emperor and, because of my own interests in the future, have utterly sold myself to him. She believes that he has won me over to him and maliciously influenced me, largely because she has seen that I do not value having Germans or people from Vienna in my house and that neither I nor my wife offers niceties to her ladies. Regarding the emperor she trusts me not at all, believing that I write or report to him everything that happens. She also harbors various prejudices against our children because, among other things, I allow my daughters to have no chamber ladies. At the moment, however, she does seem content with us and with Colloredo [Count Francis Colloredo-Walsee, tutor of Leopold's son, Francis, the future emperor], and no longer wishes to interfere in our business.

The present war [War of the Bavarian Succession] causes her

much anguish. She tells everyone that she knows nothing about it and that the emperor and Count Kaunitz, whom she has placed in charge of policy, wanted to begin the war and have deceived her in order to make the first step without advising her of the consequences. She argues to everyone that they cajoled her to make her think we were better prepared than we are and adds that she wants nothing else than an immediate peace agreement at any price so that she can withdraw from this struggle with her conscience and her scruples.

Whenever she speaks with anyone, the empress always wants to hear something new, and wishes that everyone upbraid and criticize the emperor. She constantly complains about everything and, if someone contradicts her or wants to excuse himself, she becomes angry, distrustful, and suspicious that he is in agreement with the emperor. She becomes very cross, and everyone must be most careful how he answers because sometimes she reports what she hears to the emperor himself.

My sisters Maria Anna and Elizabeth the empress treats very badly. She sees them quite seldom and almost always scolds them and displays ill temper, to Maria Anna because she always intrigues in everything and to Elizabeth because she gossips and passes everything on as soon as she hears it. The empress is especially annoyed at Maria Anna and treats her rudely at every opportunity, even in public. By and large she thinks little of Elizabeth's future [Elizabeth became abbess of a convent in Innsbruck]. Maria Anna will become a nun in Klagenfurt. The empress displays her dissatisfaction to everyone and repeats that she cannot trust either daughter and is quite unhappy with them. At every opportunity she reprimands them, even in front of people. She does not receive them in the morning, sees them almost never, and always greets them in ill humor because she suspects that Maria Anna intrigues everywhere.

The empress loves Maximilian very much, but she believes he is completely on the emperor's side and is thus totally lost and ruined by the fickleness of life—none of which is true. She utterly distrusts him, saying that he gossips quite a bit, and she believes that he is a very weak and idle individual, who undertakes nothing with enthusiasm, wants no work for himself, lives only from day to day, and will never become a great man. She worries that he repeats everything to the emperor, and so entrusts him with nothing. She values him not at all.

Finally, for Maria Christine and Prince Albert she renders the greatest affection and confidence. These two attend the empress in whatever she wants to do. They receive uninterrupted favors and the empress cannot be without them. These two, especially Maria, are with the empress the whole day, and if they are not there, they write to each other—she to the empress and the empress to her—every day, through a special courier. Maria can go to her any hour she wishes, and she alone enjoys the empress's complete trust. The empress can say anything to her, show her all her letters, notes, and documents, talk to her about everything, entrust her with anything, follow her advice, and concede to her all kindnesses. Maria receives favors and pensions, and influences the distribution of offices. If she opposes someone, he can be sure he will obtain nothing more. She constantly receives money for herself, positions and promotions for her creatures, and the most extraordinary favors. Because she effects anything she wants, makes the empress enforce anything she wishes, and interferes in all business, she can manipulate each of the empress's opinions—and the empress denies her nothing—thus dominating the empress, as well as all of her own sisters and all people. In order to please Maria, the empress helps her hold everyone in the greatest subjugation. Everyone discusses everything with Maria, especially whatever concerns the emperor. She completely controls the will of the empress, who displays such weakness and subservience toward her that she does not dare conceal anything from her or formulate anything without her. The empress does whatever Maria wants. Maria proclaims this openly, assumes herself very important, and pompously confers her protection on others. She does this so effectively that the empress fears her and not once dares to confer some favor on the other sisters without Maria's permission, lest she excite her jealousy.

15

Joseph von Sonnenfels: The Death of an Empress

One of the most interesting figures of the Habsburg monarchy in the eighteenth century was Joseph von Sonnenfels. Grandson of a famous rabbi and son of a professor of oriental languages at the University of Vienna, Sonnenfels enjoyed a varied career, serving at one time as an enlisted man in a famous Austrian regiment and then becoming professor of law and political science at the University of Vienna. During his tenure as a professor, he authored numerous textbooks for the training of noblemen entering the civil service. Because of his work, he became an adviser to Maria Theresa on many legal and educational matters and, while serving her, acquired a profound admiration for her personality and works. The following passage is a lecture which he delivered to his university classes at the first regular meeting following a recess called because of the empress's fatal illness. In this lecture Sonnenfels's feeling of grief was so great that he became choked with emotion and his listeners wept openly. Shortly thereafter numerous newspapers printed his eulogy, and later it was translated into various languages. After describing the empress's final days, at the conclusion of his address, Sonnenfels expresses in rather exaggerated terms the essence of his own political philosophy: that state and church together must control the spiritual and intellectual lives of their subjects and must insist upon devotion to the monarch as much as to God.[1]

When that most distressing order interrupted my last lecture, gentlemen, we little anticipated that the great name of Maria Theresa would be spoken from now on only with the preface "the late." Her death was as unexpected to her as it was to everyone else. But the diary of her illness, the short tale of her death, will become

---

[1] Joseph von Sonnenfels, "Die letzten Tage Theresians," in *Gesammelte Schriften* (Vienna: Baumeisterschen Schriften, 1786), VIII, 74–100. Translated by the editor.

an important contribution to the chronicles of noble reigns and of Christian heroism.

As at the death of Socrates, a Phaidon should have stood at the deathbed of this princess to write down what he saw and heard. Every word would be a lesson, every moment an example.

At the beginning, her sickness seemed only minor and unlikely to lead to serious complications. But this life had borne many children and through forty years had suffered all the fickleness of fortune which could afflict a sovereign; she experienced everything Providence uses to test the humility, steadfastness, and patience of a human being. She endured the loss of a father, a spouse, growing children, dear relatives, and a granddaughter with her name, who would have served as a reminder of the gentlest of all rulers. She has seen her subjects ravaged by long-lasting wars, torn by raging plagues and hunger, and led by false prophets from the path of truth. She has watched as her lofty intentions to create the most beneficial institutions were misunderstood and vigorously rejected by those for whose welfare they were designed. She suffered all of this disappointment with the same great sensitivity that she revealed in her warmest concern for the personal troubles of those who came to her. These disquieting circumstances made us aware that every sickness could be dangerous, and we worried that each posed a threat to her most valuable life. We knew her soul was always greater than her adversities, always independent of events and misfortunes, but the body was that of a dying person, and sixty-three years of work and trouble had not preserved it. That is what disturbed us.

We hoped to prevail upon her to use the care which had saved her earlier from more dangerous illnesses. Our prayer was fervent but largely selfish. The wisdom of the Lord had decided otherwise, and Maria Theresa's spirit seemed to have already learned her fate from a higher source. From the onset of the illness she predicted she would die; in fact she repeated it with such cheerfulness that we became convinced it would not come to pass. Her manner increased our confidence that this princess of such great piety had hardly pre-. pared herself for this important step. Ah, we did not know that she had been preparing for it for many years.

The following night, a severe blow revealed to us too soon that we had to fear for her life. The arrow of death was in her heart: its kernel of destruction was spreading—Maria Theresa, whose whole life stood as an example of the purest piety, wanted to issue her last orders to only a special following. In the morning she wished to fortify her spirit for the great journey. Her trust and vigorous faith in God overcame the weakness of her condition and supported her so that she could welcome the instrument of the Holy Ghost by receiving Holy Communion upright on her knees.

Some believed that the intense gathering of strength which followed this religious observance would revive the body and interrupt the illness. Her day was quiet, even with some evidence of her health improving, and we, who eagerly interpreted her every sign of relaxation as an improvement—which we wished so ardently— already opened our hearts to hopes. These hopes vanished forever that evening. The symptoms returned with double strength, persisted the greater part of the night, and weakened not the patience but the strength of the body so much that towards morning she demanded and received the last unction.

She understood the general grief about her, gentlemen. As the unfortunate news spread throughout the city, the laments increased. Imagine the bewilderment of those who heard the crushing report, the despair of the inner court, the hopelessness of the sons and daughters. The emperor, the archduke [Maximilian], the archduchesses Maria Anna, Maria Christine, and Elizabeth stood in a speechless circle around the deathbed and focused their grief-stricken eyes on her whom they shuddered to lose. When she had ordered all but her most intimate friends and family to leave, she turned to the emperor and said, "God has asked for my life. I feel it. Nothing that I will leave is mine; all will belong to you. Only these two daughters (she meant Maria Anna and Elizabeth) are my possessions, but even these I relinquish to you. Be not only their prince and their brother, be also their father. I leave both a rich inheritance." Joseph's love had long anticipated this command. Through the most reverent promises, he hastened to reassure her maternal concern in this hour and at least in one way to comfort his sisters over the impending loss. This pacifying step had strengthened the sibling sentiments to the utmost. The compassionate mother observed the sorrow which all expressed and finally could not bear their tears any longer. "It will be necessary," she commanded in an unchanged voice, "for you to retire to an adjoining room to compose yourselves." Only the emperor remained at the monarch's side.

This command marked the great moment in which Maria Theresa surrendered to him her empire and the nations whose good fortune until now had been the only goal of all her efforts. At this time she gave to the heir her precious testament, her earnest recommendations, and her wise memoirs. If only the contents of this solemn conversation concerning the comfort and conduct of kings could be revealed to us. These two heads of state, however, discussed without witnesses the requirements for a worthy reign and the welfare of Europe. Here it would be presumptuous to conjecture on the contents of this exchange. But none of the lessons of Maria Theresa will be lost for us. The heart of Joseph is the tablet upon which they have been inscribed deep and unerasable. We will know that the conversation of these monarchs concerned not only the government in general, but spoke of every empire, every province in particular, and likewise every nation separately. The empress made observations concerning the contents, conditions, strengths, and weaknesses of each crownland; the genius of each nation, its talents, peculiarities, and the way to handle it with a sagacity that astounded her heir and, as he himself is supposed to have declared, would have honored a Montesquieu in the hours of his clearest meditation—and Maria Theresa had but two days to live.

She devoted herself to her normal affairs and even worked with the same earnestness, patience, and constancy that she displayed at other times. She read petitions and documents, made decisions, and ratified orders. Undoubtedly one would think these last decisions and authorizations, preserved at a designated place, would reveal to foreigners and descendants both the peculiarities of the soul of this monarch, almost elevated above humanity, and of her solicitude for her subjects which she did not renounce even in the last minutes of her life.

Only the repeated seizures of the illness and her by-now increasing weakness required her frequently to interrupt her work. As soon as the pain allowed, however, and she recovered, she praised God and turned her attention back to her affairs, examining the orders she still wished to give in the future. In such quiet intervals she added from time to time various things that she wished put into her last will.

This last will, drawn up a long time ago and preserved in the private desk of this princess, is the perfect reflection of her admirable heart, full of wonderful contributions and gifts that provide either full or partial support for her charities so that they will not encounter difficulties upon her death. After the maternal provisions for the unmarried archduchesses and concern for the educational establishments, schools, and other worthy foundations, it contains a

long article in which she wills each of her trusted servants a re-
membrance. Inclusion in such a will is the most flattering reward
any servant could expect, for it represents a timeless proof of integrity included among the important documents of state and recorded forever in the archives. Whoever reads these manuscripts
will speak those names, enshrined by such distinction, with respect.

The remaining and largest portion of this last will concerned the
condition of those who were closer to the princess because of their
service and who were most affected by the fortuitous loss. This most
worthy ruler wanted to make her approaching death as easy for
them as she could. Her last testament assured to them interest for
life on the profits of investments she possessed. The emperor gave
his unconditional approval to each addition to her beneficiaries,
which should be eternally pleasing to her. She had beseeched him
to agree because those recipients whom she found worthy would
view their future prosperity not only as a legacy from her but also
as a gift of His Grace.

Amidst such labors of love of this most generous heart, death was
approaching; those who stood around the dying princess realized her
coming passing with fear and dread, whereas she who suffered received it with equanimity. Because all around her were inconsolable,
dissolved in tears, she alone was left to speak to each some word of
comfort. Death appeared to have abandoned its ghastliness within
her.

A book appropriate to the occasion was read to her. It discussed
being beyond death, a topic believed consoling when one is seriously
ill. Because she believed it true, she ordered that this passage be
read without shortening it. The reader, who until then had closed
her sorrow within her, suddenly rose and left, no longer able to
hold back her tears. "Leave, and when you have had enough of
crying, come back and continue your reading."

"You are all so afraid," she said at this moment to the crying
attendants. "I do not fear death in the least. For fifteen years I
have put my trust in Him." Shortly after awaking from a short nap,
she cried, "Do not let me sleep! I want to see death come, and," she
added smiling, "look him as straight in the eye as I can." At such
times these joking expressions are admirable.

This was not the only time she made fun of a situation which
ordinarily inspires indomitable fear in human beings. She had never
found comfort in hot rooms and preferred to keep her windows
open most of the time even in the severest winter. During this illness

she asked once to be taken to the window to breathe the cold air. The day was cloudy. "The weather," she mentioned to the emperor, who supported her, "is not the best for such a long journey." But who, may I ask, began that journey with greater courage?

She had explicitly ordered her doctor not to disguise the spread of the illness but to inform her exactly of the approach of the last hours. Concerned that he should want to spare her from it, she reminded him frequently of this command and, in the meantime, had others mention the same to him. His answers awakened more emotion in him than in the empress, who heard how little time she had yet to live.

No, I am not ashamed to admit that, with the naked recollection of this decisive moment in which she was finally taken from us, I felt the steadfastness that she did not lose even when dying. Her eyes darkened, but the cheerfulness of her spirit remained so high that she could still talk with her attendants, albeit in a broken voice. She became aware of the first spasms of death. "Are these," she asked the attending doctor, "the last, real signs of death?" "Perhaps not the last," he replied somewhat perplexed. "Ah, the last must be very hard!" That was the only complaint she uttered throughout the whole illness, the only indication that she suffered.

The burning heat that consumed entirely the small remnant of her life caused a natural motion with which she sought breath and coolness. Upon this followed a convulsive attack in her abdomen, which raised her mightily off her bed. "Where would Your Majesty like to go?" asked the emperor. She raised her glazed eyes to heaven; "to Thou above, I come" were the last words of the deceased monarch, and she sank back on the bed, supported in the arms of her son, who collected the last breath of the dying mother in a kiss. Now he gave himself to the anguish which he had so long mastered.

When he again took hold of himself, but still sunk in deep despair, he numbly looked around, and someone dared remind him of his presence of mind, which had sustained him through so many misfortunes. He replied, with a biting hint of extreme sorrow that in this situation, presence of mind simply did not apply. This answer strongly hints of what we can expect from the coming reign of Joseph.

His respect for such a dear mother and memorable ruler must undoubtedly suffer much from the resignation which he imposed upon himself not to overstep her will concerning her funeral. As she ordered, it was as devout as practical. On her command the greatest part of the splendor, which can change the burial of a ruler into a parade, was omitted.

She had expressly forbidden a funeral sermon. In her life Maria Theresa was so much against the whirl of glory hunting that she carefully avoided any ponderous praise. She did not even think of handing herself over to the flatteries of a eulogist who would feel summoned to ignore her weaknesses and exalt her virtues. He who is inclined to praise is unconcerned about the truth—the true measure of a worthy monarch is the wisdom of her administration.

Distant descendants will remember the reign of Maria Theresa for the great institutions whose purpose was not limited only to the welfare of their contemporaries. When every trace of the individual causes finally expire, the harmonizing effect will remain and will have become permanent. Then history will relate: "When Maria Theresa ascended the throne, externally Austria was without influence, without honor; internally without courage, without stability; its talents without encouragement, without emulation; agriculture in hands which misery and oppression had made limp; the government without power, without courage; commerce slight and even then conducted in the most detrimental way for the nation; and, to conclude the portrayal, the financial system without plan, estimates, or credit. At her death she relinquished to her successors a monarchy improved in the essential parts of internal administration, prepared for additional reforms, reestablished in the foremost rank of the European system, which has even assured to it the greatness and the general fruitfulness of its lands and of the fortunate national talents under its sceptre." If she did not achieve more, it was because too much was needed for one reign. But in comparing the two epochs, future generations, as this one, will call her the restorer of the Austrian monarchy.

Public and private gratitude has surpassed this sobriquet through a less practical but moving and, for the people, a more attractive name, "Maria Theresa the Good." That was the title which seemed to betray her modesty the least. Because she lay her blessings on everyone who revealed to her his needs and often obtained information about a person who could not bring himself to confess his need and thus anticipated his wishes, everyone was inclined to name charity as his favorite among her virtues.

But a few whom she particularly loved exploited this virtue. Our respect for the balanced judgment of this princess inspires us to believe that the objects of her partiality have deserved such priority.

Those who dared to oppose her decision she would have found fair, provided that the judgment of the monarch concerning this decision seemed to them in error. But some sought to conceal their envy and jealousy behind a political maxim: that a ruler should know no favorites! How terrible! What attraction could the throne have if the monarch were begrudged the taste of friendship, if he were forbidden to relax from the difficulties of office in the arms of an intimate companionship. Such a throne should isolate itself also from all affairs. Its occupant would be incapable of distinguishing merit, unable to cherish and return great devotion. He would be without feeling. How could such thoughtlessness make anyone happy?

We also add: the heart of Maria Theresa had at times been surprised. Happy is the earth if the prevailing weakness of the great is an overabundance of good. Then the people would not be crushed by the weight of their rulers' fame. The idol of conquest would remain without innocent victims and sacrifices.

The unlimited goodness of Maria Theresa, derived from the valuable but often too kindly sentimentality of her sex, is all the more wonderful because she exalted even her piety above all the petty practices of women. Her faith was earnest, but enlightened. She believed in the unrestricted progress of the soul, whose flight experiences no mournful anxiety. And her faith could not be doubted, if the undeniable evidence of natural laws could ever leave room for doubt. The education of the Church she did not leave to the claims of the clergy. Orders of this empress who is generally called a saint included exactly specified restrictions on income; prohibitions on youthful and therefore little-regarded monastic vows; proportionate contributions; and diminution of the free orders, brotherhoods, and pilgrimages. The distinguished respect, which she wanted to make the priests earn from the people, did not hinder her from establishing the exact limits which the clergy could not overstep without harming the whole condition of the institution. On more than one occasion she has shown that the humility of a worthy Christian and the power of a ruler were not contradictory and that Boniface and Gregory would have found her just as worthy an opponent as Benedict and Clement have found her a worthy daughter. But there was one issue which both sides observed carefully and which each could have violated, thereby precipitating potentially terrible consequences—an issue in which risky pretentions and interference would have created only stiffening ill will. Papal bulls that she would not officially approve, she did not burn but only let lie unopened.

Through such a calculated restraint, she anticipated the vexation of disunity between throne and altar and knew how to bring the powerful opposition to the dominance of the church into an alliance with the defense of law, which no prince had ever violated unpunished.

From this conduct, the character of the law, which Maria Theresa set against the undermining of the unbelievers, won much higher respect. Convinced that religion must sustain the worldly order, she also believed it the duty of worldly law to sustain religion. More than through the force of her laws, however, the esteem of this holy bond of the citizen body was sustained through the example of the princess. To her court and to her people, she was the model in every practice of worship, in the fulfillment of every practical duty. Her conduct taught, her behavior recommended religion in practice, and made it as charming as she was honorable.

This appealing religion was the natural impulse of all the empress undertook. It was the impenetrable shield which she threw up against all those adversities which stormed about her. It was the pillar of steadfastness at her death. When in the storm of battle the hero seems to mock death, the fog of ambition clouds him and disguises the danger in which he destroys himself, so that his courage becomes stupor. The quiet spirit, the unweakened cheerfulness of Maria Theresa as with each breath she awaited the end which would demand an account of her administration, already revealed her virtue. The great self-confidence to be able to appear without reproach before the Judge of Kings instilled in her the confidence with which she so worthily closed her famous life.

Europe will always speak the name Maria Theresa with wonder, and the nations who were fortunate enough to live under her gentle sceptre, with eternally thankful respect.

Our tribute to her will be in our application to the sciences, which mourn the death of the great donator of this chair. Nonetheless, initial signs indicate that learning will enjoy a similar protection from her successor, who must console and repair so many empires for this distressing loss.

PART THREE

MARIA THERESA IN HISTORY

> *Historians have generally viewed Maria Theresa as the savior of the Habsburg monarchy. Her determination to resist Frederick and her efforts to transform her empire into a modern state solidified Habsburg rule over the disparate lands under her sceptre and provided a strong foundation upon which the dynasty could enter the modern era. In discussing the empress, therefore, the historians represented here have tried to pinpoint that crucial characteristic of her personality or her deeds that insured her success.*

16

Hanns L. Mikoletzky: The Enlightened Despot

> *The recent head of the House, Court, and State Archives in Vienna Hanns Leo Mikoletzky views Maria Theresa as essentially an enlightened despot, both in philosophy and action, thereby conforming more closely to her fellow rulers of the eighteenth century—like Frederick the Great and Catherine the Great of Russia—than she would have cared to admit.[1]*

Intellectually, Maria Theresa was quite adaptable, which, on the one hand, allowed anyone who could make his arguments halfway plausible and who had the last word, to persuade her to accept his point-of-view, often frustrating carefully weighed decisions. On the other hand, this characteristic also encouraged a greater recep-

[1] Hanns Leo Mikoletzky, *Österreich: Das grosse 18. Jahrhundert* (Vienna: Österreichischer Bundesverlag für Unterricht, Wissenschaft und Kunst, 1967), pp. 202–4. Reprinted, and translated by the editor, by permission of the publisher.

tiveness to the problems of the day, providing, of course, that their solution in no way conflicted with her religion. She regarded the Church in the same way as Joseph I: she considered herself answerable to heaven, but not because she believed her dignity independent from all worldly origins or herself crowned "by the Grace of God" and thus responsible only to Him. In her *Political Testament*, she emphasized: "from the beginning I decided that, as my principles, I would depend upon my forthright intentions and my prayers to God; I would remove myself from all minor worries, arrogance, personal ambition, and other emotions—which I have on occasion observed in myself—and I would undertake all the necessary business of government resolutely and without passion. These maxims, with the help of God, have sustained me in my great difficulties and have made me stand firm by my decisions. In all my acts—those done and those left undone—I have chosen as my highest rule a trust in God, who, without regard to my own desires, has chosen me for this position and will make me worthy of it through my deeds, principles and intentions. Thus I felt able to solicit His help and win His almighty protection for myself and my subjects; I recalled this truth daily and it reminded me that I was responsible not only to myself but to my people. Having each time tested my intentions by these standards, I undertook everything thereafter with complete confidence, sustained mightily and yet so calmly in my soul even in the greatest emergencies, as if they did not even affect me personally. With complete tranquillity and pleasure, I would have even abandoned my whole right to rule and surrendered to my enemies, had Divine Providence so willed and had I believed it my duty or the best policy for my lands. And even though I love my heritage and my children and would spare no diligence, worry, concern, or work for them, still, when convinced in my own mind or by general conditions that it is necessary, I would always put the general welfare of my lands first because I am the foremost and general mother of all my subjects."

What Maria Theresa expressed here is nothing less than one of the fundamental maxims of the leading philosophy of her era, enlightened despotism. The intellectual movement of the Enlightenment, beginning at the close of the seventeenth century, dominating the eighteenth century, and perceiving reason as the conclusive and binding agent for all of life's aspects, had infected all aspects of civilization with optimism and confidence in the rationality of men and the universe. It had also created a specific state ethos, in which the sovereign identified with the state and, at the same time, regarded himself as its first servant. Here exists the fundamental similarity between Louis XIV and Frederick II. Supported by natural law, the ruler is obligated to employ his power unselfishly to improve the social, commercial, cultural, and political situation of his people and, concurrently, to stand above all factions and to expect the unfailing obedience of all his subjects. The sovereignty of the ruler stood united to a superior moral and legal value and was consummated in its unquestioning acceptance through the idea of *raison d'état*. In cultural affairs, tolerance and state-sponsored schools joined with compulsory education. Commercial policy was based on the idea of mercantilism. In legal matters emerged the beginnings of the state based on public justice, with the elimination of torture, abolition of secret trials, and the first great codifications of law. In administration, the principles of police protection, welfare statism, and the benefit of the general community took precedence over individual privileges. One should not overlook nor deny, however, that such governmental reforms produced important grievances. The mechanization of state and public life is a concomitant phenomenon of each perfecting system, and the administrative guardianship of the citizens, the separation of the manufacturing powers from the state, the privileges of the state-associated classes, and the suppression of unrestricted regulations in research and commerce are likewise consequences of the growth of the ideas of excessive power and order. During Maria Theresa's time, the truth of an old dictum once again became obvious, namely, that disadvantages always have their advantages: one often hears the criticism that the empress had completely unsystematic ideas. She "experimented with everything," which led to the inadequacy of many reforms and the immediate cancellation of some that had just been introduced and scarcely tried. On this account even the enlightened despotism of her era lacked the foundation of a system. Only her son would compose a detailed program, but it would destroy the necessary free flexibility that must exist in every idea. Instead of fruitful give-and-take, which guaranteed improvement and results, there stepped forth the sterilizing steel of a model. It avoided Austria, however, during Maria Theresa's reign. Here the state experimented for a long time here and there, beginning much, also achieving much, but also leaving just as much either only begun or greatly altered.

Still, one must begin and at the earliest possible moment. In one of her testaments, the empress wrote: "Since the Peace of Dresden my single goal has been to instruct myself as to the situation and potential of each province and to recognize and correct the abuses in the administration, which had thrown everything into the most decayed and damaging confusion."

17
Robert Kann: The Moderate Conservative

Largely agreeing with Mikoletzky regarding the implementation of the empress's reforms, Robert Kann, noted professor of history at Rutgers University, nonetheless differs in his opinion as to the philosophy behind them. Whereas the term "enlightened despot," in Kann's view, doubtless characterizes Joseph II, it by no means fits the personality of Maria Theresa, who in attitude was more like her father than her son.[1]

The first and fumbling stage was followed by the second, the pragmatic. This empirical feature of the Austrian Enlightenment— i.e., reform based on an assumed "social contract," let alone a rationalized popular will—is most characteristic of Maria Theresa's era. Thus in theory this period was far more clearly separated in spirit from the following doctrinaire period of Joseph II than from the preceding Carolinian regime, which had stumbled along, trying to patch up isolated cracks in the governmental system, with no thought of overhauling the whole building according to definite principles. In practice, however, this lack of comprehensive outlook in the reign of Maria Theresa's predecessor makes her own regime of widely initiated and largely completed reforms appear by comparison much more similar to that of her successor, major ideological differences notwithstanding.

The specifically constructive features of this long and respectable reign appeared far more clearly in its first part from 1740 to roughly 1765—that is, the beginning of the co-regency of Joseph. Thereafter, at first slowly and cautiously, then with increasing speed, the ideas and actions of the concentrated Josephine Enlightenment were in-

[1] Robert A. Kann, *A Study in Austrian Intellectual History* (New York: Frederick A. Praeger, 1960), pp. 121–24. Reprinted by permission of the publisher.

jected into the Maria Theresan era, and finally after taking a radical turn, they prevailed in 1780, upon the death of the empress. While it is true that the Josephine influence up to 1780 in terms of action remained rather limited, it was strong enough to change completely the spirit of the later years of Maria Theresa's reign. A steadily though haltingly developing reform movement was converted into a defensive apparatus with the chief purpose of checking the impact of the new dogmatic Josephine ideas. As for total results of the reforms, they may have differed little from those of the previous era, yet within the regime the split into a conservative and a radical trend could now be clearly discerned. Ultimately, of course, a compromise between them had to be found; but friction between the previous, rather smoothly operating middle-of-the-road policy and the impatient doctrinairism under Joseph was inevitable.

After all, Maria Theresa inherited her philosophy of government from her father. And Charles VI and many of his advisers were archconservative and (by no means necessarily a *sequitur*) highly intolerant. Maria Theresa, unquestionably far superior in achievements, would of course by modern standards be called strictly conservative in her outlook as well. This is due not so much to the comparative moderateness of her reforms and their cautious administration as to her obvious aversion to considering evolutionary administrative changes within the framework of accompanying ideological transformation. Yet important reforms were introduced after all. Thus (though with important reservations) the term "moderative conservative" can adequately describe the spirit of the regime. One of the most important reservations to the term concerns the question of tolerance. Maria Theresa was in some ways just as intolerant as her father and grandfather had been—in view of the different spirit of her times, perhaps even more so. How, then, is it justifiable to connect the spirit of the Enlightenment in the first two-thirds of the eighteenth century with the then-existing regime in Austria?

Beyond and apart from the individual will of the ruler and his advisers, social conditions forced Austria to take up many measures that in several other countries were inspired and initiated by the philosophy of the Enlightenment. The connection between Enlightenment and reform was thus transferred to the Habsburg lands, though in a reversed sense, owing to the prevalent religious atmosphere and still largely semi-feudal conditions. It was not primarily philosophy that called attention to reform; philosophy could be brought in only as the argumentative rearguard of successfully initiated reforms. However, its persuasive force was so little needed and at the same time so greatly feared that this philosophy, which had its short day under Joseph II, was again given its walking papers under his successors—something which, at least in so abrupt a fashion, did not happen to reformism itself. Thus while enlightened philosophy had only a tenuous connection with the Austrian theory of government—except during the stormy decade of Joseph II's reign and in the case of a few men before that time—it was closely linked with enlightened practice. The pragmatic reformism of the first, longer, more significant part of Maria Theresa's reign ranked with the previous rational imperialism of the expanding national empires of the generation of Louis XIV, Peter the Great, and William III. Mercantilist measures in trade, industry, and agriculture, educational reforms, revised state-church relations, in substance somewhat similar to the above-mentioned eastern and western pattern, differ from them in that their foundation was on the whole non-imperialist, and in many ways genuinely humanitarian. And this last factor, an issue worth pondering, appears more clearly in that non-intellectual, unphilosophic reign of Maria Theresa than in those of the two contemporary rulers who were deeply imbued with enlightened philosophy, Frederick II of Prussia and Catherine II of Russia.

Intellectually the equal of neither of them, Maria Theresa also cannot be held personally accountable to the same extent for the actions initiated by her advisers. But since it was she who was responsible for the approval, if not for the initiation, of her reform policy and its objectives, she deserves no mean share of the credit. This applies especially to the great centralistic reforms of her reign, in the military as well as in the civilian sphere—the only ones executed according to consistent principles. The objective of these far-reaching measures, designed primarily to strengthen the monarchy defensively, is obvious. Less obvious is the progressive consequence of these measures, which may not have been foreseen. The chief example of this is Haugwitz's comprehensive military reorganization, which in effect wrested recruiting, military financing, and equipment and supply systems from Estates' control. Thus major steps were taken toward the destruction of the feudal system. By some comparison, the far more widely acclaimed centralization of the supreme government agencies in Vienna, the organization of the state chancellery as a definite Ministry of Foreign Affairs, the clear separation of internal from external and more gradually of financial from general administration, the establishment of the commerce directory, etc., pale in importance. Of far greater significance in the long run was the separation of the judicial from the administrative functions of government, one of the few issues in which the direct influence of Montesquieu's theories on the pragmatic phase of the Enlightenment cannot be denied.

18
Eugen Guglia: The Pragmatic Reformer

One of the foremost biographers of Maria Theresa, Eugen Guglia, regards her reforms as designed exclusively to strengthen the military posture of the state. She did not centralize the administration or reconstruct the financial structure to improve the government for its own sake, but to assist the army in fighting its wars. This motive superseded all the others. In Guglia's estimation, even the major bureaucratic creation of the second reform era, the State Council, was instituted to carry on the conflict with Prussia.[1]

Maria Theresa herself cited not the Treaty of Aix-la-Chapelle, but the Treaty of Dresden as the first, deep, decisive turning point of her reign. From this treaty she also dated her first reform period. "As soon as I realized I must sign the Treaty of Dresden," she wrote in her testament of 1750–51, "I immediately changed my focus of attention and directed it solely toward the domestic affairs of my lands." As we have seen, that was not entirely correct. For at least two more years her attention remained riveted on foreign matters, namely the war with France and Spain. It is true, however, that in this same time she did concern herself earnestly with at least that problem of internal administration that is closely tied to the military and to war: a reform of finances in order to secure means for the state to fight. But once such a reform begins, it drags with it a whole series of other changes involving the relationship of central authority to the Estates, organization of the bureaucracy, commerce and industry, administration of justice, condition of the peasants and the cities, and even church and state. One change emerges from another. So the empress could say with some justification that she had to alter "the internal constitution" in order to implement the

[1] Eugen Guglia, *Maria Theresia* (Munich and Berlin: R. Oldenbourg, 1917), II, 1–2, 91, 171–72. Translated by the editor.

intended reforms in the military and finances. But it is not true that the empress and her advisers composed a great reform program according to the Enlightenment, which appeared in the second and third decades of the eighteenth century in England and France and then spread throughout the rest of Europe. They neither drew up nor systematically implemented any comprehensive program. Theory had at best a slight influence; in his memoranda Haugwitz referred occasionally to "publicists," without naming any. As models, the reformers relied only on those in Prussia, and even then only in a limited sense. All of the changes were founded on the needs of the moment and enacted as precautions to satisfy foreseeable needs at future times.

One is surprised to find that Maria Theresa, in spite of her deeds during her "heroic period" to 1748 and especially to 1745, found time for other things besides war and high politics. For instance, one would think that in the following eight years of peace, in which she turned the greatest attention to the smallest details of a reform program that encompassed all aspects of internal state administration, she would have neither the time nor the strength to concern herself with international questions, such as the relationships of the various other states of Europe to Austria and to each other. To some extent this is true: the major concern of her life in these years centered upon internal reform, and, if one follows her program, it appears as if she cared only for the internal conditions of her empire. But in fact just as she concerned herself about reform in the storm-tossed first years of her battles against her enemies, so in these years of peace every month, indeed every week, she sought to learn what her former enemies proposed, how she could strengthen her position among them, and if she could create advantageous alliances for the future. She always sought favorable conditions to reconquer or at least replace the provinces she had lost. It cannot be repeated enough that the starting point and ultimate end of almost the entire internal reform lay in the goal of improving the military strength of the empire in order to at least face every new aggressor with confidence.

During the war [the Seven Years' War] the most important new creation in the field of administration was the state council. The first occasion to inspire its creation was the financial crisis which became apparent during the preparations for the campaign of 1761.

Until then, by economizing and successful budgeting, the state had found sufficient revenues in new taxes, largely affecting Lower Austria and Vienna. But these sources of money were now exhausted; without new, energetic measures, the war could not continue. At the beginning of December, 1760, Kaunitz, at the request of the empress, set forth in a detailed memorandum (which in many ways merely repeats the contents of an earlier, unsuccessful report) the general internal situation, and judged it largely hopeless. The normal state expenditures exceeded income by about six million gulden yearly, and the total war debts had already passed one hundred million. After the peace settlement, according to Kaunitz, the army might be in such a weakened condition that it would endanger the security of the state, reduce Austria to the position of a second-rate power, and leave the monarchy defenseless against Prussia's might. Kaunitz believed the fundamental reason for these miserable conditions lay in the weaknesses of the administration which—at least in his opinion —the great reforms of the empress in 1749 had failed to remove, largely owing to the objections of the advocates of the old system like Khevenhüller. The memorandum, which obviously marked the conclusion of a series of secret talks between Kaunitz and the empress, ended with the overly optimistic suggestion that all these problems would be solved by the creation of a new bureau, known as the State Council. This council would have largely advisory duties and would receive from the empress all of her suggested measures regardless of what area of affairs they were concerned with. The empress found the estimate of the minister "nothing less than exaggerated: Our present situation," she sighed, "is fearfully critical." But she also distinguished the excessively simple solution offered by her adviser from the efficacy of his suggested reform. "With the help of this State Council and of him who suggested it to me," she said, "I believe I can prevent the ruin of the state." Later she commented, "With great expectations I await the inauguration of the new State Council as the salvation of my crownlands and the contentment of my mind and soul." As early as December 30 she appointed the members of the new central body and on January 26, 1761, the first meeting took place, with the empress, emperor, and prince of Lorraine participating.

19

Alfred von Arneth: The Too Thorough Centralizer

Alfred von Arneth, undoubtedly the greatest Austrian historian of all time, published, from 1863 to 1879, the most complete biography of Maria Theresa ever written. Despite his obvious devotion to the empress, he did not hesitate to offer his own reflections about her policies. In the following selection, Arneth, himself a nineteenth-century liberal and a critic of overmighty bureaucracies, praises the centralization of government, but he suggests that perhaps, in the long run, more benefit could have been derived from transforming the Estates into truly representative assemblies of all the people rather than eliminating their power altogether.[1]

Whoever today examines the empress's reforms impartially and with the experience accorded by over one hundred years after their implementation cannot deny his approval of the majority of her innovations. Undoubtedly, they served to remove at least partially the unjustified power of that small group of men who virtually inherited the greatest positions of the state because of their status and families and who used their offices not for the benefit of the monarch's subjects, but almost exclusively for the profit of themselves and their associates. Likewise the achievement of greater homogeneity in the administration of the individual crownlands and the removal of the administration of justice from the bureaucracy at least at the upper levels of government can only be applauded. Finally, let us not overlook the abolition of the previously decisive influence of the Estates in military affairs at a time when Austria was threatened by the rapid growth of Prussia and the concentration of its fearful power in the hands of King Frederick. In the face of this

[1] Alfred von Arneth, *Geschichte Maria Theresias* (Vienna: Wilhelm Braumüller, 1870), IV, 35–37. Translated by the editor.

danger the government had to utilize all the strength of the monarchy.

The decline of the Estates largely meant that the new offices super-
vising taxation and the military expanded their powers until finally
the Estates in Austria sank to mere shadows, the only form that the
spreading absolutist bureaucracy would allow. One can only regret
that it had to come. But one can also not deny that the Estates prepared their own fate by their own mistakes. Almost every measure
improving not only the power of the state but also the welfare of
the people encountered the most vigorous opposition from them.
Their advice almost exclusively depended on the advantages that
they would win for themselves and the privileged families, and they
opposed nothing more vigorously than an act to use the resources of
the privileged for the general betterment of the less fortunate.
Therefore, Maria Theresa and those men who enjoyed her trust
viewed the Estates not only as a challenge to justice but also as a
barrier to strengthening the state. Because the Estates always opposed measures that threatened to tax their own property for the
improvement of state interests and for the relief of the provincial
population and because they protested efforts to institute a more
reasonable distribution of responsibilities, it was natural that measures to do so should in the end be enforced without their approval
and indeed against their will. By doing so, the government finally
crushed the opposition of the Estates and removed once and for all
their decisive authority. Truly the Estates dug their graves with their
own hands.

It cannot be doubted that it would have been more satisfactory
if, instead of simply replacing the power of the Estates with the
omnipotence of the state—which truly troubled Maria Theresa—the
people themselves would have been asked to express their needs and
to participate in improving their own welfare. Only by assuring the
people's cooperation could the new order be established on a firm
foundation. But such a concept was not even considered by the most
benevolent and enlightened monarchs of the past century. They
probably agreed more or less openly with the powerful thrust of
contemporary human ideas, and they meant to do only their duty,
which they truly did, by eliminating obstacles that threatened to
hinder them. But they assumed that the enlargement of their own
power was part of the bargain and never, either in Austria, Prussia,
or anywhere else, allowed the people who were going to participate

to have any say in the new order of things. Not a single step forward occurred in this direction until finally in France, where the least was done to help the people and the most to exploit and oppress them, fearful revenge for that neglect erupted and brought with it the most violent consequences for all Europe.

While discussing Maria Theresa's reforms in the commerce and industry of the city of Trieste, Arneth raises, almost as an afterthought, a fundamental question that must be asked in any study of administrative reforms: despite reorganization of offices and changes of titles and personnel, are the problems that need solving really solved? [2]

Just as characteristic for Austrian conditions in earlier times as well as now is the importance that people always attach to the creation of new bureaucratic offices. To mention one of today's examples: confronted by the necessity of encouraging and improving agriculture, no one can think of anything better than to create a single ministry for agriculture; the same situation existed in Maria Theresa's time. If we only had a new office with a president, vice-president, so many specialists, and so many secretaries, people always say, then all of our problems would be solved.

[2] Arneth, *Geschichte Maria Theresias,* IV, 80–81.

20

Friedrich Walter: The Consummate Judge of Advisers

Friedrich Walter, a modern Austrian historian and author and editor of numerous works about Maria Theresa, attributes part of her success to her ability to choose able councilors, each of whom served her in his own special way.[1]

The second of the two great testaments, in which in the mid-1750s Maria Theresa recorded her valuable experiences regarding the struggle for the maintenance of her house and empire, and the following reform period, closed with the sentence, "The most important concern of a ruler is the selection of his advisers." This quotation is almost the cardinal insight of the first decade and a half of her reign, which this great monarch and lady wished to impress upon her "beloved successors" as the most important lesson for rulers.

Because "it pleased her father never to instruct her in the business of domestic or foreign affairs," on his unexpected death she found herself in the most difficult situation of depending completely on the ministers then in office. She knew neither their human peculiarities nor their professional talents. She had no choice but to work with her father's old councilors, but she realized their weaknesses only too soon.

Among them, Count Philip Louis Sinzendorf, the Austrian court chancellor, stood as undisputed leader in rank and esteem. He conducted "the business of the house and diplomacy" and, thanks to his experience spanning over a generation, enjoyed decisive influence. But despite the sympathy that she tried to muster for him, her opinion of her first minister was truly unfavorable. "Although, while

[1] Friedrich Walter, *Die Paladine der Kaiserin* (Vienna: Bergland Verlag, 1959), pp. 5–11. Reprinted and translated by the editor, by permission of the publisher.

he served her, she could never confront him with it," she harbored
the serious suspicion that he was being bribed by the Prussians and
that he had entered into a corrupt agreement with them concerning
the rape of Silesia. And it appears that her doubts regarding his
incorruptibility were not completely groundless. These suspicions,
however, probably were only secondary for the young queen, for her
opinion centered on the count's belonging to the considerable party
that believed it inevitable that the queen should "consent to negotiate" with Frederick II. At that time and later as well, Maria Theresa
judged people on the basis of their attitude toward Prussia; she
viewed people and events largely from the point of view of the
Silesian question. In the case of Sinzendorf, it became obvious that
the man had scarcely more than mediocre talent, which could not
long deceive the incisive perception of the queen.

The generally important and troublesome financial ministry was
the realm of the aged Count Gundacker Thomas Starhemberg. He
enjoyed the unlimited trust and hearty respect of Maria Theresa.
Agreeing completely with the young queen in matters of foreign
policy, he possessed a rich knowledge of all fields of finance, and
with this solid attribute, which he owed to the unflinching honesty
of his thirty-five-year-long directorship of the Bank of Vienna, he
shored up the often sagging confidence in the financial structure of
the state. When Maria Theresa assumed the throne, however, he was
seventy-seven years old and "no longer as active" as the troubled
times demanded he be.

Next to Sinzendorf and Starhemberg, Count Philip Joseph Kinsky
had the temperament and talent to be influential. Not in the best
interests of the state nor of the queen, he combined with unquestion-
able gifts and unusual adaptability an irritable temper and "a violent and brusque manner," which occasioned many quarrels and
much discord. Especially injurious was his rough, particularistic,
provincial attitude, his "protection for his nation which he endeavored to favor regardless of anything else." Moreover, his moodi-
ness made him susceptible to frequent changes of mind, which once
prompted Maria Theresa to admonish him, "Why such an attitude,
why such a face? Do not discourage your poor queen more, but help
and advise her."

With such hands on the helm, who was going to guide the pitch-
ing ship of state out of the storm of battle against a world full of
enemies and into a safe harbor? This ministry was a collection of
short-sighted, easily discouraged, and largely senile and exhausted

men, who gave up the queen's cause as lost before the struggle had even begun. At the beginning of July, 1741, when the court was in Pressburg on the way to celebrate the coronation of Maria Theresa as queen of Hungary, news arrived of the alliance treaty signed the month before between France and Prussia. At that time, as the English ambassador reported home, "The ministers fell back deathly pale in their chairs; only the queen herself remained steadfast." Maria Theresa recorded this event in the same way. "Without vainly seeking fame, I can testify that I alone (although undoubtedly not because of my own virtue but thanks to the grace of God) displayed the required courage in the face of all these blows."

The empress is too modest when she, out of the thankfulness of her devout heart, overlooks her own efforts and views as God's work the fortunate dissolution of the iron ring around her inheritance. After all, God helps those who help themselves. She never expected a miracle, but, trusting in Providence and the righteousness of her cause, she worked day after day, week after week, month after month, and year after year.

God could not deny His approval of such work, and He made His favor evident by sending to this brave woman those helpers whom she needed if she would achieve her supreme goal, the undiminished retention of her crowns.

At the beginning of her reign, the afflicted queen needed a man who would carry to the hoped-for successful result her decisive refusal to sign any treaty of virtual surrender with Prussia; she found him in Bartenstein. Experienced and assiduous, true and courageous, upright and moral, he became the vigorous defender of the policies of his queen-empress in those first difficult years. Soon after securing Bartenstein's devoted service, she won a fatherly friend in Silva Tarouca, who fulfilled his function by giving his opinion—not always in pleasant fashion—concerning all that she did or allowed. With the gravity of his words, he tried to boost her self-esteem and fortify her willingness to assume responsibility. Primarily he gave her spiritual strength, which she needed to persist in the battle for the internal rejuvenation of the monarchy. She manifested this gift of courage almost immediately in a bold move: following Silva Tarouca's suggestion, she chose as leader of the great reform a previously unknown middle bureaucrat of the Silesian administration and installed him, despite the bitterest opposition, at the head of the domestic policies of the realm. This man was Haugwitz. It was his great achievement that out of a bundle of variously formed and variously acquired sovereign lands brought together in a territory of the greatest natural and cultural dissimilarity, divided by parochially loyal political Estates and held together only by the person of the monarch, he created a new, centrally ruled, modern state. His work laid the foundation upon which Kaunitz, like Haugwitz appointed directly by the empress herself, based his audacious foreign policy which turned the European diplomatic order upside down. Kaunitz created the diplomatic prerequisites for the renewal of the battle for Silesia in which the strength and power of France and Russia were employed in a "great coalition" to serve Austria's interests. Even though he was in the end incapable of retaking Silesia, he still raised the world's respect for Austria—a respect squandered in the last years of Charles VI—to an unprecedented height.

If Silesia remained Prussian, the reason was above all in Maria Theresa's failure to find a general who could match the military ability of Frederick. Even Daun, the victor at Kolin and Hochkirch, was not his equal. But still he was the best that Austria could send into the field. And when later [Gideon Ernest] Laudon's star began to rise and [Francis Morris] Lacy's high military ability and organizational talent became known, the empress managed, through her unflinching reconciling efforts, to overcome the personal friction and animosity within this triumvirate and make possible a harmonious cooperation which restored the old glory of Austrian arms. The great reforms, undertaken after the end of the war of succession, can be considered largely, although not exclusively, as the renewal of the material strength of Austria, with the final goal being a military effort to reconquer lost Silesia. In a broad sense, however, it [the reform period] was an end in itself, particularly in the spiritual-cultural realm. The general decline, into which the monarchy had fallen in the second quarter of the eighteenth century, had also gripped intellectual life, especially education. To have instituted fundamental reforms and to have selected the right man to try to inject new blood into the desolate high schools and to widen the restricted intellectual horizons through a censorship favorable to learning were special achievements of the empress, especially since she never possessed a deep appreciation for the learning and spirit of her age. The intellectual-cultural stimulus in Maria Theresa's time is intimately linked with the name of [Gerhard] van Swieten. The empress originally brought him to Vienna because he was a renowned doctor, but from the beginning his work far exceeded merely caring for the physical well-being of the imperial family.

And even though the intellectual world, whose frontiers Van Swieten sought to expand, remained largely closed to Maria Theresa, she nonetheless bravely defended his work against the assaults of all the little obscurantists.

These then are only the heroes who played the major roles in that drama of events that unfolded under the empress on the Austrian stage. Next to the Bartensteins and Haugwitzes, Kaunitzes, Dauns, and Van Swietens, stood many men, to whom the script allotted scarcely an appearance, allowing us only a casual glance, before sending them back into the shadows.

We are familiar with this whole polymorphic, constantly changing world not only from the arid manuscripts of the voluminous provincial bureaucracies and central offices or the numerous letters of the empress and her children, but in the complete and colorful diary of Khevenhüller, who through thirty-five years had stood near his beloved sovereign in life and in service. With the devotion of a chronicler, he tells of his daily work, of major and minor events, and of the many people whom he encountered—admittedly mostly of the great aristocracy. In his sketches exist moving testimony of the deep love of this great woman for her husband and many enlightening glances into the difficult relationship between the mother and her firstborn son after she appointed him coregent. If marriage was to her an inexhaustible fountain of happiness, so was the way which she had to tread as mother of this son, stony and thorny—and yet, after her husband, no one stood closer to her than Joseph, and for hundreds and hundreds of reasons she was enormously proud of him and loved him passionately.

Above all, her whole being with all its love belonged to the husband, who was only average in ability. Next she loved her son, who although equal to her at least in his quick understanding, never reached the depth of her feeling. Yet she stood above all the men around her, ruling as much through her genial talent for government as through her wonderful womanliness. Certainly this or that man surpassed her in knowledge of particulars, but no one contested her in the overview of the whole or the accuracy of decisions in particular regarding the requirements of general policy. She was not infallible; she remained embarrassed by many errors all her life and repeatedly encountered problems she could not comprehend and realized her ignorance of many things. With many of these men she struck up a profound friendship—a friendship of the mind and heart—she surrounded them with womanly care, and mildly and intelligently saw beyond their weaknesses. And she never forgot a single favor. She achieved what no other great woman of world history had achieved: she became an excellent sovereign, without concurrently betraying her womanhood, and she was always a woman without forgetting her imperial dignity. As queen-empress, she was above all "universal and first" mother of her lands.

21
William Coxe: The War Leader

The first author to compose a comprehensive study of the Habsburg monarchy in English was the Anglican clergyman William Coxe. Relying primarily on the reports of the British ambassadors in Vienna, he largely ignored the internal reforms, preferring instead to examine the diplomatic and military events in which Maria Theresa often appears only incidentally. In the following selection, however, he stresses the importance of the empress in fortifying her subjects' will to resist and provides a detailed and interesting account of the battle of Kolin, the first Austrian victory over Frederick the Great. In honor of this success, the empress awarded to her commander in chief, Field Marshal Leopold Daun, the Order of Maria Theresa, which became one of the highest honors in the Austrian army. In the first paragraph Coxe refers to the battle of Prague, in which Frederick defeated an Austrian army commanded by the empress's brother-in-law and which set the scene for the encounter at Kolin.[1]

Thus victory was declared on the side of the Prussians, but was purchased by the loss of their best troops, not less than 18,000, even by the avowal of the king, being killed, with many of his bravest officers, and Schwerin, the father of the Prussian discipline, and the guide of Frederic [*sic*] in the career of victory. Of the Austrians 8,000 were killed and wounded, 9,000 made prisoners, and 28,000 shut up within the walls of Prague. The defeat would have been still more complete had prince Maurice been able to pass the Moldau, and intercept the fugitives; but the river having risen, he had not a sufficient number of pontoons to form a bridge, and a column of

[1] William Coxe, *History of the House of Austria*, 3rd ed. (London: Henry Bohn, 1854), III, 375–79.

16,000 Austrians made good their retreat along the Moldau to join the army of marshal Daun.

Prague was instantly blockaded by the victorious army, and not less than 100,000 souls were confined within the walls, almost without the means of subsistence. They were soon reduced to the greatest extremities; but the spirit of the troops and of the inhabitants was animated by an address from Maria Theresa, brought by a captain of grenadiers, who escaped the vigilance of the besieging army.

"I am concerned," said the empress, "that so many generals, with so considerable a force, must remain besieged in Prague; but I augur favourably for the event. I cannot too strongly impress on your minds, that the troops will incur everlasting disgrace should they not effect what the French, in the last war, performed with far inferior numbers. The honor of the whole nation, as well as of the imperial arms, is interested in their present behaviour; the security of Bohemia, of my other hereditary dominions, and of the German empire itself, depends on a gallant defence, and the preservation of Prague. The army under the command of marshal Daun is daily strengthening, and will soon be in a condition to raise the siege; the French are approaching with all diligence; the Swedes are marching to my assistance; and in a short space of time, affairs will, under the divine Providence, wear a better aspect."

This address, from a sovereign whom they adored, excited general ardour; the garrison, though reduced to feed on horseflesh, held out with uncommon perseverance; and the inhabitants supported without a murmur all the horrors of a bombardment, which destroyed one quarter of the town. Several desperate sallies were made; but the garrison was threatened with famine; and the loss of Prague would have been followed by the most fatal consequences. The recent defeat had spread consternation throughout Germany; the elector of Bavaria and the other Catholic princes had already sent agents to treat with the king of Prussia; and almost every member of the empire was preparing to desert the cause of Maria Theresa. The flower of her armies was shut up in Prague; the remainder defeated, dispirited, and dispersed; the capital of Bohemia reduced to the last extremity; the whole kingdom ready to submit to the law of the conqueror; her hereditary dominions exposed; Vienna itself threatened with a siege, and the imperial family about to take refuge in Hungary.

In this disastrous moment the house of Austria was preserved from impending destruction by the skill and caution of a general, who now, for the first time, appeared at the head of an army. This general was Leopold count Daun, a native of Bohemia, son of Wyrich Philip Lorenzo count Daun and prince of Tiano, who had distinguished himself in the campaigns of Italy during the reigns of Joseph and Charles, and had held the high offices of viceroy of Naples, governor of Milan, and stadtholder *ad interim* of the Netherlands. Leopold was born in 1705, embraced the military profession at an early period, and learned the art of war under Seckendorf and Khevenhüller. He distinguished himself at the battles of Crotzka, Dettingen, and Hohenfriedberg; and from his knowledge of tactics, was chosen to introduce the new system of discipline into the army. Although favoured by Eugene and Khevenhüller, he had risen slowly and silently by merit, and without intrigue, from a subaltern rank to that of field marshal; and after the death of prince Piccolomini, was intrusted with the army, which, under his auspices, was to restore the honor and credit of the Austrian arms. Sagacity and penetration, personal bravery tempered with phlegm, animation in the hour of battle, with extreme caution both before and after the engagement, recommended him at this critical juncture, like another Fabius, to check the fire and enterprise of the modern Hannibal.

On the first intelligence of the entrance of the Prussians into Bohemia, Daun had marched through Moravia towards Prague, to effect a junction with prince Charles. On arriving at Boehmischgrod, within a few miles of Prague, he was apprised of the recent defeat, and halted a few days to collect the fugitives, till his corps swelled so considerably, that Frederic detached against him the prince of Bevern with 20,000 men. Daun, though superior to the enemy, was too prudent to hazard the fate of the house of Austria on the issue of a single battle, with dispirited and almost desponding troops, against an army flushed with recent victory. On the approach of the prince of Bevern, he therefore retreated to Kolin, Kuttemberg, and Haber, in order to afford a refuge to the shattered remains of the defeated army, and to receive the recruits which were pouring in from Moravia and Austria.

While he was thus baffling the enemy, he, like the great general who saved Rome by delay, had to support the murmurs of his officers, and the reproaches of those impatient spirits who are always eager to engage and cannot distinguish prudence from pusillanimity. Among others the duke of Württemberg exclaimed, "If you continue this conduct, I would advise you to march to Vienna; but I will retire to my own dominions, and countermand the troops I have ordered to join you." Yet neither invectives nor murmurs could induce Daun to change his wise measures, until his army was increased, and the soldiers began to recover from their despondency. Finding himself at length at the head of 60,000 men, he made a rapid movement in front, forced the prince of Bevern to retire, and was advancing to attack the king in his posts before Prague, while prince Charles was to make a sortie with his whole force.

Frederic, conscious of his danger, had already anticipated the design of Daun; leaving the greater part of his army to continue the blockade, he marched with 12,000 men on the 13th of June in the morning, and joined the prince of Bevern on the 14th, at the moment of his retreat before the Austrians. On the approach of the Prussians, Daun occupied the heights stretching from the village of Chotzemitz towards Kolin; he placed his infantry on the flanks, which were supported by steep eminences, filled the villages in his front with detachments of infantry and irregulars, stationed the cavalry in the centre where they could act with effect, and made a skillful disposition of his formidable train of artillery.

In this situation Daun was attacked by the king of Prussia, who, directing all his efforts against the Austrian right, had almost succeeded in turning their flank, notwithstanding their superiority of number, the tremendous fire of the artillery, the skill of the general, and the bravery of the troops. Victory seemed to incline to the enemy, and Daun had even ordered a retreat; but the fortune of the day was changed by the impatience of two Prussian generals, who, disobeying positive orders, broke their line on the right to dislodge a party of Croats, and were repulsed with considerable loss. The Saxon cavalry instantly rushed into the interval, crying out at every stroke, "Remember Strigau!" and cut to pieces or dispersed all whom they encountered. Daun availed himself of this fortunate maneuvre with equal skill and promptitude; he was seen flying from rank to rank, animating the soldiers by his voice and gestures; he had two horses killed under him, was twice slightly wounded, and showed himself the worthy antagonist of the great Frederic. In vain the king of Prussia exerted all his skill and courage in this desperate conflict; his cavalry charged six times, and were six times repulsed; Frederic again rallied them, and finding them dispirited, exclaimed, "Would you live for ever!" They were a seventh time led to the charge, and were again driven back. Perceiving the battle lost, the king ordered two regiments of cuirassiers to disengage the infantry;

but discouraged by the dreadful carnage of their companions, they refused to advance. He then sullenly withdrew from the field with a squadron of gardes du corps, and thirty hussars; and was repeatedly heard to cry out, "My hussars, my brave hussars, will all be lost!" The troops also, for the first time defeated, gave way to despondency, and in their retreat exclaimed, "This is our Poltava!" Daun purchased the victory with the loss of 9,000 men; but on the side of the Prussians not less than 14,000 were killed, wounded, and taken prisoners; and 43 pieces of artillery, with 22 standards, fell into the hands of the Austrians.

Maria Theresa, who was anxiously waiting the event of an engagement, which, if unfortunate, would have rendered her situation more deplorable than that to which she had been reduced at the commencement of the former war, received the account with a joy proportionate to her apprehensions. Sumptuous feasts were given, medals struck, and presents distributed; the officers were rewarded a month's pay, and the subalterns and common soldiers were gratified with donations. Anxious to display her gratitude to the general who had first defeated her formidable antagonist, she conveyed, in person, the news of this important victory to the countess Daun, and instituted the military order of merit, or the order of Maria Theresa, with which she decorated the commander and officers who had most signalised themselves, and dated its commencement from the era of that glorious victory.

22
Heinrich von Srbik: The German Queen

The leading Austrian proponent of the "German-Imperial" school of history, which reached its height in the period between the First and Second World Wars, Heinrich von Srbik saw Maria Theresa as the embodiment of Austrian-German womanhood.[1]

How had the fortune of the truly great historical power in the middle of Germany and the continent fared, while England and France ranged around the globe and Prussia rose to European prominence? A truly great woman had reproduced, although in a confined way, the old Habsburg-universal idea; she had created a new German esteem and had, at the same time, given her own state new forms of life and power. A lasting symbol of the German type, a child of the great heritage of her house—of its ideas and works—and, concurrently, a newly created individuality: such was Frederick's great opponent. In her person and in her state she embodied that powerful life-thrust of the German people, grown on non-German soil, venerable and yet new. Maria Theresa and Austria pointed the way into the future as did Prussia and Frederick the Great. The historian, who tries to understand the deepest trends of German fortune, must dwell thoughtfully on the nature of this sovereign and her state.

The daughter of the last Habsburg, the fresh and strong bloom of life on the ancient and defoliated Habsburg tree, will stand for all time before the eyes of succeeding generations as a human, immensely attractive example of self-sacrificing womanhood. She had the beauty of a noble heart; she was a warm-blooded, upright, and truly sensitive human being, even in her weaknesses. In her also lived a heroic, courageous, and steadfast soul and strong will, which

---

[1] Heinrich von Srbik, *Deutsche Einheit* (Munich: F. Bruckmann, 1935), pp. 107–11. Reprinted and translated by the editor, by permission of the publisher.

enabled her to battle heroically for her rights and inheritance. She was no philosophical spirit like the enemy of her life. Her thought was generally interlaced with sensitivity: instinctive, elementary, housemotherly, and matriarchal. She was a German woman by descent and inclination and was knowingly proud of her Germanness, but burgeoning Austrian awareness grew in her one of its most beautiful buds. Quite mistaken in its understanding of this German Austrian nation is the opinion that the Habsburg Counter Reformation castrated forever the inheritors of the German colonizing genius and forever weakened German spirit and character. Indigenous and inexhaustible German power and primeval customs had still remained in the Alpine and Sudeten lands. In her simplicity, her warmth of heart, and her open, natural disposition, Maria Theresa was both a German and Austrian woman; she was also an Austrian woman in her unsystematic and illogical method of thought, in the primacy of her feeling, her aversion to all abstraction and mechanization in her ideas and in her sense of the tangible, national, and natural; Austrian also in her stability in misfortune, in her generosity, her good nature, her enjoyment of life, and in the musical rhythm of her being. As Frederick gave Prussianism its particular stamp, so has Austrianism preserved to the utmost the characteristics of this great German and Austrian princess; retained also Maria Theresa's tender way of handling people and political affairs and her natural insight into the art of the possible. In the natural unity of her important inheritance, she embodied and strengthened the Austrian nature, German in blood and substance and yet influenced by foreign blood, able to absorb foreign ways, cheerful, colorful, naturally impulsive, and full of worldly sense, open to foreign cultures and educating them through its own higher cultural life. This Austrian nature became a singular worthy fruit on the luscious tree of German totality. Suited like no other for the problems of Central Europe, Austria was a "cultural unity of European Christianity—seen as German." If north German intellectuality found its highest expression in Herder and Kant, the musical, Catholic Austria of the eighteenth century produced its most beautiful German cultural blood in Gluck, Haydn, and Mozart. As in the uppermost state administration and national policy, the basis of Maria Theresa's cultural affairs was also German.

She did not disavow the family-dynastic appearance of Habsburg cosmopolitanism, tied to the medieval-imperial idea and maintained in ever-weaker forms since the great ancestor Charles V and once

again revived in the Spanish experience of her father. Truly fem-
inine, she furnished her sons and daughters with German bishoprics,
with thrones and governorships from Belgium and Milan to the
Bourbon royal court in Paris, and felt herself the great mother of a
wide-ranging world. She felt proud of the history of her house,
proud of the new, Europe-encircling bonds of her offspring, and true
also to the Catholic-universal character of the old Habsburgs and of
the Holy Roman Empire, whose protagonist she truly was in spite
of everything. Throughout her life she remained personally loyal to
the religious period of German history, but still had gradually
bowed to the spirit of the Enlightenment. She preserved the Habsburg belief in the mission of her house, and, like Charles V and unfortunately like her father, she stood by the belief in the sanctity of
rights and treaties in international affairs. But she also knew clearly
and thoroughly how to restrict her policies to the realities of the
political world in Central European and German affairs. Her purpose was above all the struggle to retain the leadership of Germany
not only for her dynasty, but also for her monarchy in the Holy
Roman Empire, a struggle against the approaching dualism, a struggle for the imperial crown and for Silesia, the cornerstone of that
particularly German power of Austria. She also fought a moral
battle against unbridled power and state egotism. She had secured
again for Habsburg-Lorraine the chairs of the imperial bishoprics;
she had secured for her husband the imperial crown, had engineered
the imperial coronation of her oldest son, and had maintained for
Austria at least first place in the empire and kept the holy crown
which her forefathers had worn for centuries, even if she could not
retain her state's premier position among the great powers. She had
also recruited the best talents from the empire for the external and
internal improvement of her state affairs and, through the charm
and greatness of her personality, had inspired in the German people
a spirited example of heroism in contrast to the cold courage of
Frederick the Great.

As already mentioned, Maria Theresa bore a strong German
awareness in her; she valued her German people as the most virtuous of all. With national delight, she mentioned that Hungary
would be conquered and pacified "only with German blood," and
she loved this German people. In this female offspring of the old
house, the imperial idea was no longer truly a deep, spiritual force.
Maria Theresa had envisioned the imperial crown so much as the
natural attribute of her house's power that she did not fear to lead

the revolt against the legal rights of Charles VII, who had truly become emperor by the grace of France and Prussia and was the enemy of her rights of succession. By doing so, she effectively weakened the prestige of the imperial crown. The conflict of Austria and Prussia made it clear that for both opposing German powers "the empire" and the office of emperor no longer stood as independent terms, but as the objects of rival coalitions. Under the bitter pressure of German great-power dualism, the time of the Roman-German imperial idea, incorporated much more deeply into the blood and history of Austria than of Prussia, went into decline as it already had under Charles VI. The idea of the Danubian state pressed forward with elemental force.

23

Henry Marczali: The Good Hungarian

A prominent Hungarian historian at the turn of the century, Henry Marczali, points out that the primary change in Hungary during Maria Theresa's reign was not the incorporation of its political power into the bureaucracy in Vienna—indeed the empress's reforms had minimal effect— but the attitude of the Hungarians themselves, who no longer despised their monarch as an alien sovereign but regarded her a woman after their own heart.[1]

Much less complete than the Catholic victory over Protestantism in Hungary was the triumph of the King's authority over the Estates in Parliament. The *jus resistendi* (the famous right of rebelling against the King with impunity) had been abolished in 1687; the hereditary succession to the throne had been assured in that year and in 1723; the ordinary taxes, the recruits and military supplies, the charges for transport and quarterage had been voted by Parliament. During the closing years of her reign Maria Theresa had found it possible—by an evasion of the laws indeed—to rule for fifteen years without calling a Parliament, to dispense with a Palatine, and to rule through a lieutenant-governor; in no case had any resistance been offered. More than this, it had been possible to regulate the financial obligations of the serfs against the wishes of the nobles, to compel the prelates to pay taxes for the upkeep of the frontier-fortresses, and to determine, and even to decrease, the number of begging friars and of feast-days; it had even been possible to alter the whole system of national education with success and without any disturbance of importance. None the less, in the most essen-

---

[1] Henry Marczali, *Hungary in the Eighteenth Century* (Cambridge, England: Cambridge University Press, 1910), pp. 324–27. Reprinted with permission of Cambridge University Press.

tial points the older society had managed to maintain its existence. If their serfs did pay war-taxes, the nobles were exempt from all burdens, for, as they put it themselves, their "shoulders" were "virgin." The comparative ease with which the nobles and the clergy were induced to consent to a diminution of their authority as against that of the King, was due to the fact that in the age of Maria Theresa the idea of a State was as yet indistinguishable from the hierarchy and aristocracy. The orders could show compliance to an ally, and they did not consider the sovereign as their enemy. Further, though there was no Parliament nor Count Palatine, the county—i.e., the executive power—still remained the intact and undisputed domain of the old system of administration.

As regards the destruction of national feeling, scarcely any perceptible headway had been made. Not only members of Parliament and of the county assemblies, but those attached to the Royal Chancellery and to the *consilium locumtenentiale*—in fact all who were by birth Hungarians—never forgot their native country even when confronted with the royal power. Numerous laws had been successfully modified, but one fact remained at all times valid, namely, that Hungary—being an independent State—could not be governed in the same manner as the Hereditary Provinces of Austria. So strong was this feeling, nay even so omnipotent, that it was sooner or later bound to override any and all other considerations, and to destroy or to modify the influence of foreign institutions opposed to national tendencies. Thus, though the sovereign's Court had proved an excellent means of welding the various elements in the Habsburg "Empire" into one, we find that the Hungarian nobles attended it at Vienna only to further the interests of their own country and nation, despite all the enchantments of the Great Queen. What great things Maria Theresa expected from the Hungarian noble bodyguard! The latter did indeed serve to spread culture, but it made its character primarily Hungarian. An important political object in the organisation of the national education had been the spread of the German language. The organisation was preserved, but it served above all to further the development of the Hungarian language and literature. On this inspired soil patriotism was the prophet, and those profane people who met him were forced, in the image of the legend, to converse and prophesy in company with him.

This national feeling actually permeated both the Catholic Church, elsewhere so cosmopolitan in character, and the equally universal "caste" spirit of the nobility as well. All conquests won by the former were made not only for the faith but for the nation too; and all that the latter succeeded in preserving was a national gain. Though much was done in the age of Maria Theresa to encourage and prepare the way for a centralisation of the monarchy, it was very rarely that measures were taken which in any way injured Hungarian national feeling. Any act of the sovereign who had established a Hungarian bodyguard, founded the Order of St. Stephen, built palaces at Buda and Pozsony, annexed the "Banat," Fiume, and the towns of Szepes to Hungary, abolished the independent Rascian administration, and declared and shown herself on all occasions to be a good Hungarian—any act of hers might have been condoned. No Hungarian could have protested against the impersonation of the unity of the "Empire" by such a figure. Hungary, which at the beginning of the century, with cries of *eb ura fako* ("Hands off, Austria!"), had desired to break away from the King and to form an aristocratic republic like that of Poland, was now distinctly monarchical in feeling. She desired no Polish liberty, but looked to the sovereign for all good:

> I would say—and you must comprehend me—
> If you would live a happier life,
> Pray zealously and speedily to the King of Heaven
> To send this world good sovereigns.

So we can understand—however unfamiliar the tone may be to us— the desire of Revay, that the Empire of the double-headed eagle should spread far eastwards; and we can comprehend the lines of John Gyongyosi of Transylvania, who wrote:

> May the eagle take under his wing what now is the Turk's;

We find nothing strange in the fervent hymn of Baron Lawrence Orczi:

> Now is the beginning of a golden age,
> Emperors have become the fathers of their dominions.
> Kings are the mates of good citizens,
> And great lords consort with poor peasants.

Afterword

Upon her death, Maria Theresa was succeeded by her son, Joseph II, who immediately implemented the sweeping reforms he had tried to persuade his mother to accept. Within a year after her death, he issued both an Edict of Toleration, allowing Protestants and Greek Orthodox a measure of religious freedom, and a Patent to Abolish Serfdom, guaranteeing freedom of person to every peasant. Joseph then instituted a thorough centralization of the monarchy by obliterating all traditional and provincial divisions, introduced extensive changes in law and judicial procedure, abolished all monasteries and convents that failed to serve social needs, and decreed equal taxation for all citizens. During the ten years of his reign, he issued over 6,000 edicts, covering virtually every matter of concern to himself and his subjects. To Joseph II, the state existed to ensure "the greatest good for the greatest number," and no customs, institutions, or sentiments were going to prevent him from achieving that goal.

Unfortunately for Joseph, however, his wholesale changes did not create a state of satisfied citizens but elicited instead an outburst of protest against him. Upon embarking on a war with the Ottoman Empire in 1788, Joseph found himself confronted by threatened revolution in Hungary and open rebellion in Belgium. Stunned by these outbursts and warned of seething discontent elsewhere in the monarchy, Joseph revoked many of his reforms. In February, 1790, he died, convinced that he had utterly failed.

Historians often compare the reigns of Maria Theresa and Joseph, emphasizing essentially the mother's unsystematic approach to reforms and the son's thorough, logical completeness. Undoubtedly Maria Theresa's changes were introduced in haphazard and often contradictory fashion, leaving many gaps and including frequent half measures. But her reforms were always thoroughly pragmatic. Believing in no rigid philosophy or blueprint for action, she introduced innovations where she thought they were needed and to the degree she felt necessary to achieve the desired result. She judged a reform by its practicability, not by its logic, and by its effect on her subjects and the state, not by its abstract rationality. She recognized the need for caution and prudence, two characteristics not found in her son. Consequently, she experienced no serious outbreak of opposition from any of her provinces or from any stratum of society.

Undoubtedly Maria Theresa was the best loved of the Habsburg monarchs in the early modern period of European history. She was courageous and indomitable and, at the same time, generous and kind. She respected the rights of others and fully expected others to respect hers. While cautious in making decisions, once taken she was resolute in their implementation and openly expressed deep irritation at any delays. Although often critical of her ministers, she never tried to ruin them or humiliate them publicly, and those who served her loyally, even if not well, earned her undying gratitude. In intellectual and artistic matters, her vision was limited, but, except in religious affairs, she never tried to force those around her to limit their perspective to accord with hers. These characteristics, plus her natural grace and charm, inspired in her people a loyalty to the Habsburg monarchy that stood it in good stead for the next century and a half. When she came to the throne, her state appeared on the brink of dismemberment; when death took her from it, her state had been restored to the front rank of the modern European powers.

Bibliographical Note

This bibliography by no means includes all of the works about Maria Theresa. Rather, I have listed books in English on various aspects of her reign and state and have included the more important titles in German when it was warranted by the merit of the book or the lack of an English source.

Biographies

In the last few years Maria Theresa has become the subject of a number of biographies in English, which in many ways make up for the absence of such studies prior to the 1960s. Of these recent works, the most thorough is Edward Crankshaw, *Maria Theresa* (London, 1969). Robert Pick, *Empress Maria Theresa: The Earlier Years, 1717–1757* (New York, 1966) presents Maria Theresa as a popular figure but, in doing so, overlooks much of the latest historical research on various aspects of her reign. Probably the best but also the shortest of the recent biographies is C. A. Macartney, *Maria Theresa and the House of Austria* (London, 1969), which clearly summarizes the various reforms within the government.

Of the older biographies, the most important remains Alfred von Arneth, *Geschichte Maria Theresias* (Vienna, 1863–1879), the ten-volume masterpiece upon which most subsequent biographies are based. This work not only offers details of the empress's life and work but also contains many original documents, published in their entirety. Other valuable biographies in German include Eugen Guglia, *Maria Theresia* (Munich, 1917) and H. Kretschmayr, *Maria Theresia* (Leipzig, 1938). The older studies in English are by and large disappointing; these include Constance L. Morris, *Maria Theresa, the Last Conservative* (London, 1938); Margaret Goldsmith, *Maria Theresa of Austria* (London, 1936); J. A. Mahan, *Maria Theresa of Austria* (New York, 1932); and James F. Bright, *Maria Theresa* (New York and London, 1897). Although inadequate as a biography, G. P. Gooch, *Maria Theresa and Other Studies* (London, 1951) contains much information concerning the empress's relations with Joseph II and Marie Antoinette, and offers translations of many letters that passed between them.

General Histories

General histories of the Habsburg monarchy in English are few, but once again a number of recent studies have done much to fill the void.

Victor S. Mametey, *Rise of the Habsburg Empire, 1526–1815* (New York, 1971) provides the essential facts of the monarchy's history during the time designated by the title and includes a bibliography of works in English. Another useful source is C. A. Macartney, *The Habsburg Empire, 1790–1918* (London, 1968), which, notwithstanding the first date in the title, offers much information about the administrative, demographic, and social structure of the monarchy during the eighteenth century. An excellent study of the Habsburg family is Adam Wandruszka, *The House of Habsburg* (Garden City, N.Y., 1964), a short but interpretive work covering the whole 600-year history of the dynasty. In German, the two best general histories are Erich Zöllner, *Geschichte Österreichs* (Vienna and Munich, 1966) and Hugo Hantsch, *Die Geschichte Österreichs*, 2 volumes (Graz, Vienna, and Cologne, 1962). Hanns Leo Mikoletzky provides an interpretive survey of the eighteenth century in *Österreich: Das grosse 18. Jahrhundert* (Vienna and Munich, 1967) but unfortunately includes no bibliography.

Source Books

A number of editors have compiled selections from the writings of Maria Theresa, but few of these have been published in English. Maria Theresa's first *Political Testament* and a smattering of other letters can be found in C. A. Macartney, ed., *The Habsburg and Hohenzollern Dynasties in the Seventeenth and Eighteenth Centuries* (New York, 1970) and various letters to her children in the above-mentioned volume by Gooch. Of the recent collections in German, probably the best is Friedrich Walter, ed., *Maria Theresia: Briefe und Aktenstücke in Auswahl* (Darmstadt, 1968). An excellent edition of the empress's two political testaments, which reveals the great difficulties in interpreting them, is Josef Kallbrunner, ed., *Kaiserin Maria Theresias politisches Testament* (Vienna, 1952).

Biographies of Other Personalities

Of the individuals surrounding Maria Theresa, Joseph II has received the most attention from biographers. The old standard English work by Saul K. Padover, *The Revolutionary Emperor* (New York, 1934) has been largely superseded by the more critical but brief Paul P. Bernard, *Joseph II* (New York, 1968) and T. C. Blanning, *Joseph II and Enlightened Despotism* (New York, 1971). Still, however, the best study of Joseph remains Paul von Mitrofanov, *Joseph II. Seine politische und kulturelle Tätigkeit*, 2 volumes (Vienna and Leipzig, 1910). Of the other members of Maria Theresa's family, an excellent study of Leopold is Adam Wandruszka, *Leopold II*, 2 volumes (Vienna and Munich, 1965). Works on Francis Stephen include Fred Hennings, *Und sitzet zur linken Hand: Franz*

Stephan von Lothringen (Vienna, Berlin, and Stuttgart, 1961) and Hanns Leo Mikoletzky, *Kaiser Franz I Stephan und der Ursprung des Habsburgisch-Lothringischen Familienvermögens* (Munich, 1961). Despite a number of recent studies, the best work on Maria Theresa's youngest daughter remains Stefan Zweig, *Marie Antoinette* (New York, 1933).

Nonfamily figures in the empress's court have received scant attention from English authors. Aside from *A Study in Austrian Intellectual History* (New York, 1960) in which Robert Kann presents a good analysis of Joseph von Sonnenfels, none of Maria Theresa's advisers has been the study of a significant biography. Neither Haugwitz nor Kaunitz has attracted a good recent work in German, although the latter has been the subject in G. Küntzel, *Fürst Kaunitz-Rittberg als Staatsmann* (Frankfurt, 1923) and A. Novotny, *Staatskanzler Kaunitz als geistige Persönlichkeit* (Vienna, 1934). Major works concerning other individuals include F. Silva Tarouca, *Der Mentor der Kaiserin* (Vienna, 1960), a study of Silva Tarouca by one of his descendents and F. von Thadden, *Feld Marschall Daun* (Vienna, 1968). Friedrich Walter provides excellent short biographies of the important individuals in *Männer um Maria Theresia* (Vienna, 1951), republished in 1959 as *Die Paladine der Kaiserin*.

Particular Studies

No works in English adequately examine Austria prior to Maria Theresa's succession, although some information can be gleaned from Nicholas Henderson, *Prince Eugene of Savoy* (New York, 1964), a biography of the great Austrian military figure who died in 1736. The diplomatic aspect of Austria's war with the Turks from 1737 to 1739 is presented in Karl A. Roider, *Reluctant Ally: Austrian Policy in the Austro-Turkish War of 1737–1739* (Baton Rouge, La., 1972). In German, probably the best works discussing Austria before 1740 are Oswald Redlich, *Das Werden einer Grossmacht: Österreich, 1700–1740* (Vienna, 1938) and the superb five-volume *Prinz Eugen* (Vienna, 1963–1965) by Max Braubach.

For Maria Theresa's early administrative reforms, see Friedrich Walter, *Die Geschichte der österreichischen Zentralverwaltung in der Zeit Maria Theresias, 1740–1780* (Vienna, 1938) and by the same author, *Die Theresianische Staatsreform von 1749* (Vienna, 1958). No good work in English exists on the Habsburg army, but Gunther Rothenberg, *The Military Border in Croatia, 1740–1881* (Chicago, 1966) provides an excellent look at the institution of the *Grenzers* in particular and a good bibliography of military affairs in general. For economic matters, see the article by Hermann Freudenberger, "Industrialization in Bohemia and Moravia in the Eighteenth Century," *Journal of Central European Affairs* XIX (1960), 347–56 and the book by Gustav Otruba, *Die Wirtschaftspolitik Maria Theresias* (Vienna, 1963). Otruba's work contains a valuable bibliography on all aspects of the empress's reign. Of all her reforms, the serf issue has received the most attention from English-speaking authors. Edith M. Link, *The Emancipation of the Austrian Peasant* (New York, 1949) examines serf reform in Austria; and William E. Wright, *Serf, Seigneur, and Sovereign: Agrarian Reform in Eighteenth-Century Bohemia* (Minneapolis, 1966) discusses the same question in Bohemia. Legal changes can be found in Henry E. Strakosch, *State Absolutism and the Rule of Law: The Struggle for the Codification of Civil Law in Austria, 1753–1811* (Sydney, 1967).

For a discussion of the impact of the Enlightenment on Austria, see Robert Kann, *A Study in Austrian Intellectual History* (New York, 1960) and Paul P. Bernard, *Jesuits and Jacobins* (Urbana, 1971), although the latter deals far more with the age of Joseph II.

Works in English on the various provinces of the Habsburg monarchy are few. Those most important include Béla K. Kiraly, *Hungary in the Late Eighteenth Century* (New York, 1969); Henry Marczali, *Hungary in the Eighteenth Century* (Cambridge, England, 1910); and Robert Kerner, *Bohemia in the Eighteenth Century* (New York, 1932). For Belgium, see the study in German by Heinrich Benedikt, *Als Belgien österreichisch war* (Vienna, 1965) and for Italy, the same author's *Kaiseradler über dem Apennin: Die Österreicher in Italien, 1700 bis 1866* (Vienna, 1964).

Index

183